Praise for
Southern INSPIRED

"Ever since we saw Chef Jernard compete in the finals of *Food Network Star*, we knew he would be on TV for many years to come. Jernard's work ethic is second to none."

—Jon Steinlauf, chief US advertising sales officer of Discovery, Inc.

"*Southern Inspired* is a delicious collection of recipes and stories personally curated from my friend Jernard Wells. His new cookbook is for everyone who enjoys cooking, and I personally love the way he puts a soulful touch on each dish, from Italian to Mexican, while still paying homage to his southern roots! He is celebrating American Food from his experience, and every recipe is wonderfully packed with flavor and loaded with history."

—Melba Wilson, owner of Melba's Restaurant in Harlem, New York City

"A popular phrase is KISS: keep it simple, stupid. When you read Chef Jernard's cookbook you realize he has put a twist on the phrase and it's KISF: keep it simply fantastic! Chef Jernard delivers an easy-to-use cookbook that I'm happy to tell everyone I'm using in my kitchen!"

—Rushion McDonald, two-time Emmy Award–winning executive producer and CEO of 3815 Media

"Every single page of *Southern Inspired* is packed with delicious recipes and stories that inspire us all to celebrate our roots. You can feel Chef Jernard's personality and dedication to his craft throughout the book. His larger than life personality, his down home easy approach to making food that has inspired him throughout his culinary journey, and his ability to put his signature Southern spin on everything he touches make him one of today's hottest celebrity chefs. He has the full package and takes great pride in making sure he feeds your mind, body, and soul. He is the truth, and you will want to make every single recipe. This hot new book shows you just why Chef Jernard Wells is one of today's hottest Southern Chefs in the culinary game!"

—Rochelle Brown and Sonia Armstead, Executive Producers, New Soul Kitchen, Powerhouse Productions

Southern
INSPIRED

Also by Chef Jernard A. Wells

*88 Ways to Her Heart: "Cooking for Lovers"
from the Kitchen to the Bedroom*

*Southern Modified: Southern Inspired Dishes,
Modified for Today's Healthier Lifestyle*
(with Denise Boutté)

Southern
INSPIRED

More Than 100 Delicious Dishes from My American Table to Yours

CHEF JERNARD A. WELLS

Written with Dana Slusarenko

Photography by Jensen Taylor
Food Stylist: Francesca Zani
Culinary Assistant: Corey L. Hinton
Culinary Contributor and Super Mom: Gwendolyn Willis
Culinary Consultants: Rochelle Brown & Sonia Armstead
Recipes developed, tested, and shot at PowerHouse Test Kitchen

BenBella Books, Inc.
Dallas, TX

BenBella Books, Inc.
10440 N. Central Expressway
Suite 800
Dallas, TX 75231
benbellabooks.com
Send feedback to feedback@benbellabooks.com

BenBella is a federally registered trademark.

Printed in the United States of America
10 9 8 7 6 5 4 3 2 1

Library of Congress Control Number: 2022013474
ISBN 9781637741504
eISBN 9781637741511

Editing by Claire Schulz
Copyediting by Karen Wise
Proofreading by Marissa Wold Uhrina and Sarah Vostok
Indexing by WordCo
Text design and composition by PerfecType, Nashville, TN
Cover design by Brigid Pearson
Cover photography by Jensen Taylor
Printed by Versa Press

Special discounts for bulk sales are available. Please contact bulkorders@benbellabooks.com.

Contents

CHAPTER 7
Veggies for Life

CHAPTER 8
Wings and Things

CHAPTER 9
On the Side

CHAPTER 10
Brunch

CHAPTER 11
Desserts to Die For from My Momma's Kitchen

CHAPTER 12
Sippin'

CHAPTER 13
Holiday

Foreword

FOOD IS SUCH AN ESSENTIAL PART OF OUR CULTURE—AND GOOD food represents so much more than a meal. Our ancestors' resilience and creativity are exemplified by the selection of ingredients in many of the dishes we enjoy as traditional cuisine and sacred family recipes. Some of our fondest memories and most profound decisions are made as we break bread with family, friends, and colleagues. It's how we express love, innovation, community, and fellowship. Those among us who take the art of cooking and use it to extend our heritage, culture, and contribution to society are artisans - just like Chef Jernard Wells.

Chef Jernard holds a special place in my heart. I have spent some of my most profound moments with this talented young chef at my kitchen table, where he shared not just his love of cooking but also his heart. As he whipped up some of his signature dishes, like Southern Sweet Tea Brined Fried Chicken accompanied by sauteed cabbage and turkey bacon, I would sit across the table admiring his passion for his craft and enjoying the stories of his journey. His incredible cooking style and flair for flavor take me back to my own roots—reminding me of the delicious veggies and spices plucked from my home-grown garden and crab legs sourced from the waters in my own backyard. I admire and respect his passion for taking what's old and making it new again while challenging us to embrace new food experiences like our ancestors of old. From his Chunky Buffalo Cauliflower Bites to Jackfruit and Rice-stuffed Pineapples, Chef Jernard is not afraid to merge ingredients and flavors to create a fusion of simple yet unique dishes that dazzle our taste buds. His effervescent personality and infectious smile also make him hard to ignore. His latest book, *Southern Inspired*, will introduce you to the stories and recipes I have grown to know and love about Chef Wells, and they will bring you back for more.

Jernard and I have bonded over great food - an excellent bridge to a great relationship. Ironically enough, it was as he was cooking up one of his great recipes that we discussed the idea of putting him in front of the Urban One audience. Now, Chef Jernard is a staple on cruises for our radio listeners and a popular figure on CLEO TV's *New Soul Kitchen* and *New Soul Kitchen Remix*.

I am incredibly proud of Chef Jernard for using his passion and gift for cooking as his vehicle to impact the world. I am grateful that he and his beautiful family have connected with me and mine, personally and professionally.

Chef Jernard, keep being great and always remember that humble beginnings start in the heart and will take you all around the world.

Cathy Hughes
Founder & Chair
Urban One, Inc.
(Radio One, TV One, Cleo TV, IOne Digital & Reach Media)

GREW UP IN A LARGE SOUTHERN FAMILY WHERE FOOD WAS AT THE center of our home and community celebrations. It didn't matter if it was a birthday party, backyard barbecue, or a wedding; food was the guest of honor. And my parents, grandparents, and great-grandparents gave me the most meaningful education in food starting when I was a child. Every Saturday, I watched my great-grandmother, Mrs. Lizzie Mae Young (whom we all called Lil Momma) prepare feasts of sun tea-brined fried chicken, juicy grilled pork chops, cast iron corn bread, Dagwood sandwiches filled with freshly smoked meats and cheeses from our smokehouse on the farm, glazed strawberry lemon cake, and her irresistible banana pudding. Lil Momma used to say to me, "Nardi" (she called me Nardi), "You have to make sure you *feel* a certain way before you even step foot into the kitchen to cook." She didn't have to explain what she meant. It was a lesson as great as any technique or cuisine theory I would ever learn: your intention and emotions flavor your food *as much as* any herb or spice ever could.

Lil Momma made everything on Saturday because Sunday mornings were spent loading up her picnic baskets with Tupperware containers of "goodness" before heading off to church. Now, in the South our services used to last for what seemed like forever—maybe three or four hours, which is a lifetime for kids. Lil Momma knew that to keep me and my sisters from complaining, she'd have to feed us at some point. And just when we thought we couldn't take it anymore, the service would end and out came the Tupperware—green lids, yellow lids, orange lids—I always knew where to find my favorites! Then we'd eat, forgetting that our toes were pinched in our dress shoes and our necks were scratchy from our church clothes. I never knew that cold chicken could taste so good! But it wasn't just the food itself; it was the love my great-grandmother infused into her food that made it taste so delicious. It was the love!

Over the years, I developed an appreciation and respect for the food we ate. I learned how the Southern classics my family cooked had originated and how critical these foods were to the foundation of what we call American cuisine (I'll get to that again in just a few pages). But more importantly, I saw how food brought people together, broke down barriers, built fellowship, and cleared the way for love to take hold.

My Culinary Journey

As a chef, I speak through food and food speaks through me. Cooking for me has always been about the four F's: faith, family, food, and fun! I come from a big family with a long line of chefs and entrepreneurs. Food was, and still is, the cornerstone of who I am and how I've lived my life.

At the 2020 Taste Awards in Los Angeles with my sister Shannon; my mom, Gwendolyn; and my brother Adam when I was inducted into the Taste Hall of Fame.

Everybody has an origin story. It doesn't matter who you are or where you're from—everybody started from somewhere and has a story to tell. Sometimes life is familiar and predictable, and other times you think life is taking you down one path only to discover that your destiny lies elsewhere. Take my origin story, for example. Even after I started college, I believed that I was going to be a lawyer. That's right, the "Chef of Love" (a nickname from my

Southern Inspired

early years as a teen chef), Attorney-at-Law! If there's one thing that I want you to know, it's this: I didn't choose food, food chose *me*. Let me take you back . . .

One of my favorite shows to watch when I was a kid was reruns of the 1960's comedy series, *The Beverly Hillbillies*. Man, I loved that show! It centers on a man named Jed Clampett, who picked up his family and moved from the rural hills of the Ozarks to Beverly Hills, a city with swimming pools and movie stars. Our family made its

I loved visiting with my grandparents, Lizzie Maye and Peter in Mississippi, on our family farm. As a kid, I spent many of my summer days running around the fields and gardens and working with my grandfather.

own cross-country journey. But unlike Jed, my dad, Matt, picked up his family from Chicago—a city with deep-dish pizza and Oprah—and moved us to Michigan City, Mississippi, a down-home, deeply Southern town with dirt roads and cotton fields. Talk about culture shock! But right there is where my journey really started.

You see, we moved to Mississippi to help tend to my great-grandparents' farm. They had some 200-odd acres full of cattle, hogs, chickens, soybeans, corn, and various vegetable crops. There I learned the value of hard work and the meaning of "salt of the earth" communities. It was also the place where I developed an appreciation for fresh fruits and vegetables and grew to understand the importance of knowing where our food comes from and how that can impact our health. I didn't know it at the time, but the foundation for my career was being laid!

From about the age of 10, I spent a lot of time in the kitchen with Lil Momma. She and my mom, Gwen, had so much fun cooking that I wanted some of *that* for myself! Our kitchen was always filled with laughter and the most intoxicating smells that would make your knees buckle just waiting to see what would come out of the oven or off the stove. It was from them that I learned the value of a well-seasoned cast iron pot, as well as stories about our culture and history as a family, how we came from former slaves, Apache chiefs, and yes, some Irish too. My mom would say to me, "Nardi, you have to learn how to cook because you don't know if you'll ever get married and you gotta know how to take care of yourself." At least that's what she said, but looking back on it, she might have seen something in me that I didn't see in myself at the time: a budding love for food and an understanding of how food connects us all.

But it wasn't only my mom and great-grandmother who introduced me to the magic of cooking. My dad, Matt, was an entrepreneur and cook himself. He would have me right by his side as he spent hours cooking and packaging meals to sell to the community. I can still smell that hickory wood from the smokehouse we had on the farm, how it would get into our clothes and cling

Me and Keena on our wedding day on June 25th, 1999. That day, not only did I get married to my true love, partner, and biggest cheerleader, but I also made the food for our celebration!

Southern Inspired

to us like a smoky souvenir, allowing us to relive the joy of the day as we cooked brisket, ribs, and ham for hours at a time. And my dad and I would just talk, not about anything specific—just enjoying each other's company. I realized later that was our time to be together, father and son. Those were some of my fondest memories from growing up.

When I was 16, my dad passed away. I knew our lives had changed, and I didn't want to burden my mom with all the things a 16-year-old boy wanted (namely, a car). So, I figured I'd make some money doing something that I already knew how to do and was pretty good at: cooking. I went to my mom with $50 in my pocket and told her I wanted to open a restaurant. Gwen looked at me like I was crazy and said, "Where are you going to open a restaurant with $50?" I told her, "Your kitchen!" My mom didn't skip a beat. She told me to dust off the encyclopedias that I had never cracked open and come up with a business plan. When she got home that night, I handed her the proposal, and the next day she took me down to City Hall to get a business license. After a lot of laughs and snide remarks, I left that office with my license in hand!

My Mississippi Love BBQ Lasagna (page 10) will become your go-to recipe in a heartbeat.

Long story short, by the end of that summer I was making $3,000 a month cooking! I continued my business until I graduated from high school, but I didn't recognize it as a career for myself because I had always believed that I was going to be a lawyer. Even though I really loved what I was doing—and was making money doing it—I couldn't see it as my future.

It wasn't until I was attending Rust College in Holly Springs, Mississippi, majoring in political science—because I was going to be a lawyer,

This picture was taken in All New Deli, my first brick-and-mortar in Holly Springs, Mississippi, where the menu featured some of my favorite sandwiches and Southern meals.

remember—that my eyes were opened, and I stepped into my destiny. It was there that I bought my first brick-and-mortar restaurant in my freshman year, right across from the campus. A year later, I would graduate from the Memphis Culinary Academy and the rest, as they say, is history. A history spanning the last two decades as an executive chef and restaurateur with TV appearances across numerous networks, and culminating in hosting my own signature TV shows, *New Soul Kitchen* and *New Soul Kitchen Remix* on CLEO TV—but I've only just begun!

So that's my origin story. And through the stories I heard from my mom and Lil Momma, I learned that cuisines have origin stories too. Cultures blend and borrow from each other as they evolve to create unmistakable dishes. American cuisine is the epitome of such blending, as we are a nation built on diversity. But American food wouldn't be what it is today without Southern cuisine—especially the cuisine of the African American cooks whose contributions came to define it.

American Cuisine Took Root in the South

You can't tell the history of America without acknowledging the pain, struggle, and contributions of formerly enslaved Africans, just like you can't have what we call American cuisine without acknowledging the contributions of African American cooking as a building block in its foundation, despite its heinous origins.

Southern Inspired

Foods that were brought to America by enslaved Africans include rice (specifically, Carolina Gold), okra, black-eyed peas, yams, watermelon, kola nut, leafy greens, coffee, sorghum, and millet. Our grace as a people lies in our respect for these foods—how they nourished our bodies and, in turn, connected us to our past and to each other as a community. Cooking techniques such as barbecuing, and dishes like gumbo and jambalaya, have been woven into American culture and cuisine, but all have roots in Africa.

Throughout my life I've learned that one of the biggest myths in the culinary world is that "soul food" is only African American food—separate from American cuisine. This is a stereotype. What I know for certain is that the "soul" in soul food is the feeling, the love, the joy that you experience when eating or cooking food that touches you to your core. Simply put, it's cooking from the heart.

There would be no American cuisine without the "soul" inspired by enslaved Southern cooks, and *my* cooking style was built on that legacy.

Southern Inspired

I believe that food has always brought us together and that breaking bread with one another is a universal expression of love and community. I hope you'll welcome me into your kitchen as we journey across borders with recipes inspired by my Southern roots—from regional classics like Creole Red Beans and Rice and Shrimp and Sausage Étouffée to creative new favorites that represent the stages of my culinary journey like Blackened Salmon with Coconut Cream Crawfish Sauce and Black and Pink Peppercorn Crusted Petite Filet with Whiskey Glaze. Join me as I share easy-to-follow recipes like Mississippi Love BBQ Lasagna, Lollipop Drumsticks with Whiskey Chipotle Sauce, Lemon Pepper Chicken Skewers, Jackfruit and Rice Stuffed Pineapples, and "Brown Sugar Baby" Peach Cobblers. With chapters devoted to vegetarian dishes, a backyard barbecue, a holiday feast, and more, *Southern Inspired* has something for everyone!

I hope sharing these dishes brings you as much joy as I felt creating them. I promise you that I've put as much love into this collection as if I was cooking for Lil Momma herself. Enjoy!

Chef Fernard

CHAPTER 1

BRINGING IT
Home

THE WORD *HOME* OFTEN EVOKES FEELINGS OF COMFORT, LOVE, closeness, and familiarity. Why do you think so many common phrases draw meaning from its usage? Homestyle, homesick, down-home, there's no place like home, home sweet home—the list is endless. Part of what makes a house a home are the connections and memories that develop as families grow—many of which are rooted in shared meals and celebrations.

My siblings and I were blessed to have grown up in a home with loving parents who helped shape us while gifting us with lasting memories—many of them connected to joyous times spent around our table. But my mom, Gwen, was truly the backbone and driving force in our family. She didn't let anything hold her back from achieving her dreams and embracing her passions. She worked in the entertainment industry before switching to nursing. All the while, she had channeled her long-held love for baking—so when she retired from nursing after 28 years, she became a pastry chef!

It takes a certain type of cleverness to teach people when they don't know they're learning, and Gwen had that gift. She planted seeds when I was distracted and taught me lessons when I wasn't paying attention—seeds and lessons that grew into the foundation of the chef I am today.

One of Gwen's lessons cemented itself as a cornerstone in my cooking style: "Take something you really love and bring it into your world, make it uniquely yours." The first time she inspired me with this piece of wisdom was when I saw her make Mississippi Love BBQ Lasagna. As I watched her blend traditional lasagna ingredients—flat noodles, crushed tomatoes, oregano, and parsley—with our family recipe barbecue sauce and smoke-house cheeses, it all made sense. It didn't hurt that she baked that bad boy to perfection in her trusty cast iron skillet over our wood-burning stove out back. But don't worry, I've modified this recipe so you won't have to go out and chop wood for the fire. Your oven will do just fine!

It's said that you can't go home again, but I think you can—if just for the time it takes to finish a meal made with one of these nine uniquely inspired dishes from my childhood. There's always a place for you at the table.

And always listen to your momma!

Mississippi Love BBQ Lasagna | SERVES 6–8

THERE'S ONE PHILOSOPHY AROUND FOOD that was instilled in me as a child that I've carried over into my career as a chef. That is to draw inspiration from my Southern roots as an African American and balance those culinary traditions with those of other cultures and flavors. In other words, take what you know combined with what you admire to create familiar yet unique flavors—and Mississippi Love BBQ Lasagna is just that! Here, I take a cue from my mom and blend traditional lasagna ingredients with sweet barbecue sauce and use four kinds of cheese— ricotta, Parmesan, smoked provolone, and smoked mozzarella—to give this dish a smoky and tangy quality yet unmistakable lasagna flavor. Your taste buds will thank you!

Southern Inspired

3 tablespoons olive oil

6 garlic cloves, minced

½ cup small-diced yellow onion

½ cup small-diced green bell pepper

Kosher salt

Cracked black pepper

1 pound ground beef

8 ounces mild ground Italian sausage

3 cups your favorite barbecue sauce

7 Roma tomatoes, crushed

2 teaspoons dried oregano

32 ounces whole-milk ricotta cheese

¾ cup grated Parmesan or Romano cheese, divided, plus more for garnish

1 pound no-boil lasagna noodles

2 cups shredded smoked provolone cheese

2 cups shredded smoked mozzarella cheese

Chopped fresh flat-leaf parsley, for garnish

1. Preheat the oven to 350 degrees F. Have ready a 9 × 9-inch or 9 × 13-inch baking pan.

2. Heat the oil in a large cast iron skillet or sauté pan over medium-high heat. Add the garlic, yellow onion, and green bell pepper and season with salt and pepper as desired. Sauté until the onion is translucent and the pepper is soft, 3–4 minutes.

3. Add the ground beef and sausage and cook, breaking up the meat with the back of your spoon and mixing it into the vegetables, until it begins to brown, 10–12 minutes. Season again with salt and pepper as desired.

4. Lower the heat to medium and add the barbecue sauce, crushed tomatoes, oregano, ricotta, and ½ cup of the Parmesan cheese. Stir to combine so that the cheeses begin to melt into the sauce.

5. To assemble the lasagna, spread a generous spoonful of the sauce in the bottom of the baking pan. Cover with an even layer of lasagna noodles, then spoon more sauce on top. Sprinkle with some of the provolone cheese, some of the mozzarella cheese, and the remaining ¼ cup Parmesan cheese. Continue to make layers until you have reached the top of the dish, ending with sauce, provolone, and mozzarella.

6. Cover the lasagna with aluminum foil and bake for 40 to 45 minutes (for a 9 × 13-inch pan) or 30 to 35 minutes (for a 9 × 9-inch pan). Remove the foil and continue to bake for another 15 minutes or so, until the lasagna is golden brown and bubbly.

7. Remove the lasagna from the oven and let it set for 10–15 minutes. Top with chopped fresh parsley and serve with more Parmesan, if you like.

Chef Jernard's Crackin' Seafood Boil | SERVES 8–12

ALTHOUGH THE ORIGINS OF THE seafood boil may be questioned by some, and the bragging rights for the best version may be contested among the Gulf Coast, New England, Mid-Atlantic, and Lowcountry varieties, there's one thing for certain—a seafood boil is guaranteed to bring a celebration to your table! When I was growing up, our boils were a community affair. Just like moths to a flame, our neighbors knew it was time to make their way to our house when they caught a whiff of those Cajun spices mingling with the shrimp, crab, crawfish, potatoes, and corn—all they needed to do was bring an ingredient to drop in the pot to keep the party going! I'm not suggesting you do the same, but it couldn't hurt!

---

3 quarts cold water

2 quarts chicken broth

2 lemons, halved

2 large yellow onions, quartered

2 garlic cloves, peeled

¼ cup kosher salt

¼ cup crushed red pepper

¼ cup black peppercorns

3 tablespoons Cajun seasoning, homemade (page 20) or store-bought

5 sprigs fresh thyme

4 bay leaves

2 pounds tricolored new potatoes

5–6 ears corn, husked and halved

2 pounds smoked sausage links, cut into 1-inch pieces

2 pounds crawfish

5 pounds jumbo shrimp, peeled (tails left on) and deveined

4–5 pounds Dungeness or snow crab legs

---

1. Combine the water and chicken broth in a 6–8-quart heavy-bottomed pot. Squeeze the juice from the lemon halves into the pot, then drop them in. Add the onions, garlic, salt, red pepper, peppercorns, Cajun seasoning, thyme, and bay leaves, and bring to a boil.

(continued)

2. Add the potatoes and cook over medium heat for about 5 minutes. Add the corn and cook for an additional 5 minutes. Add the sausage and cook for another 5 minutes. Add the crawfish and cook for 5 minutes. Add the shrimp and crab legs and cook until the shrimp turn pink, about 5 minutes more. Check to make sure the potatoes, vegetables, and meat are cooked through and tender.

3. Take the pot off the heat, carefully drain off the liquid, and serve with crab-cracking sauce (recipe follows).

Crab-Cracking Sauce

8 tablespoons (1 stick) unsalted
   butter
2 cups your favorite hot sauce
½ cup minced garlic
¼ cup light brown sugar
2 tablespoons chili powder
2 tablespoons garlic powder

2 tablespoons onion powder
2 tablespoons lemon pepper
1 tablespoon Cajun seasoning,
   homemade (page 20) or
   store-bought
1 teaspoon cayenne pepper

1. Melt the butter in a small sauté pan over medium heat. Add the remaining ingredients, stir to combine, and bring to a boil. Remove from the heat and serve warm.

Southern Inspired

Momma's Chicken Pot Pie | SERVES 4–6

THIS IS ONE OF THOSE DISHES that warms your bones just thinking about it—but it might seem intimidating because of the daunting task of mastering a homemade crust. I wouldn't think of having you miss out on this kiss of comfort, so I've used store-bought puff pastry to give you a hand. And to enhance the depth of the creamy filling, I've added just enough Cajun seasoning and pink peppercorns to give you that warm and fuzzy feeling.

½ cup avocado or olive oil

1½ pounds boneless, skinless chicken breasts and thighs, cut into 1-inch pieces

2 medium potatoes, peeled and cut into ½-inch pieces

2 medium carrots, small diced

2 medium celery stalks, small diced

8 ounces green beans, trimmed and cut into ½-inch pieces

1 cup fresh or frozen sweet peas

2 garlic cloves, minced

2 tablespoons Cajun seasoning, homemade (page 20) or store-bought

⅓ cup all-purpose flour

2 cups low-sodium chicken broth

1½ cups heavy cream

1 teaspoon whole pink peppercorns

4 scallions, thinly sliced, plus more for garnish

2 tablespoons chopped fresh flat-leaf parsley leaves

1 tablespoon fresh thyme leaves

Kosher salt

Cracked black pepper

1 sheet frozen puff pastry, thawed

1. Preheat the oven to 400 degrees F. Have ready four large ramekins or a 9 × 13-inch baking pan.

2. Heat the oil in a large, heavy-bottomed saucepan over medium-high heat. Add the chicken and sauté until almost cooked through, 5–7 minutes. Add the potatoes, carrots, celery, green beans, sweet peas, and garlic, and mix the

(continued)

vegetables in with the chicken. Season with the Cajun seasoning and sauté until the vegetables begin to soften and the chicken is fully cooked, about 5 minutes. Using a slotted spoon, transfer the chicken and vegetable mixture to a large bowl, keeping the oil and drippings in the pan.

3. Turn the heat to medium and add the flour to the pan, whisking it into the oil. Cook, stirring constantly, until a blond roux forms, 5–7 minutes. You want to make sure the raw flour taste cooks out. Add the chicken broth and whisk to get rid of any lumps. Whisk in the heavy cream. Add the pink peppercorns, scallions, parsley, and thyme and season with salt and pepper as desired. Bring the sauce to a light simmer over medium-low heat and cook until the sauce has thickened. You will know when desired thickness is reached when there is minimal dripping from the back of your wooden spoon.

4. Return the chicken and vegetables to the pan and stir to combine with the creamy sauce. Cook for 1–2 minutes.

5. Transfer the filling to the ramekins or baking pan. If you're using ramekins, cut the puff pastry into 4 individual pieces and lay one over the top of each ramekin. If you are using a baking pan, cover it with an entire piece of puff pastry.

6. Bake on the middle rack for 20–25 minutes (for individual ramekins) or 30–35 minutes (for a large pot pie) or until the puff pastry is golden brown and the filling is bubbly. Remove from the oven and allow to cool slightly. Sprinkle with more scallions and serve right away.

Blackened Catfish
with Smoked Gouda Grits | SERVES 4

FIRST INTRODUCED TO BRITISH COLONISTS by Indigenous peoples and subsequently embraced by enslaved African cooks, grits have transcended the stereotype of modest Southern food to now grace the menu pages of fine-dining restaurants across the country. But the true magic of grits lies not just in its versatility but also in its ability to evoke joy and nostalgia. My Blackened Catfish and Gouda Grits recipe takes me back to the warmth I felt as a child when my parents worked together—Gwen stirring the pot and Matt tending to the cast iron skillet—as they prepared bowls of cheesy grits topped with perfectly blackened pieces of catfish for me and my siblings. I knew it was created from love, and it tasted like a mouthful of hugs!

1½ teaspoons Cajun seasoning, homemade (page 20) or store-bought
1 tablespoon smoked paprika
1½ teaspoons chili powder
1 teaspoon cayenne pepper
4 (8-ounce) catfish fillets, each cut into 2–3 pieces

Kosher salt
¼ cup olive oil
4 tablespoons (½ stick) unsalted butter
2 teaspoons garlic powder
Chopped fresh flat-leaf parsley, for garnish

---

1. First, start the grits (recipe follows). These will hold while you cook the blackened catfish.

2. To make the blackening seasoning, mix the Cajun seasoning, smoked paprika, chili powder, and cayenne pepper together in a small bowl.

3. Season the catfish pieces on both sides with salt and blackening seasoning.

4. Heat the olive oil in a large cast iron skillet over medium-high heat. Right before adding the catfish to the skillet, add the butter and let it melt—do not let it burn. Add the catfish to the skillet in a single layer. Sprinkle some

(continued)

garlic powder on top and sear for 3–4 minutes, then flip the pieces over, sprinkle the other side with garlic powder, and sear for another 3–4 minutes. The spices should form a dark crust on the outside, and the fish should be opaque and flaky inside.

5. Serve the catfish over the grits, garnished with chopped parsley.

Smoked Gouda Grits

2 cups water
2 cups chicken broth
2 cups quick grits
4 tablespoons (½ stick) unsalted
   butter
Kosher salt

Cracked black pepper
1 tablespoon light brown sugar
2 teaspoons garlic powder
½–¾ cup canned coconut milk
1½–2 cups shredded smoked Gouda
   cheese

1. In a medium saucepan, bring the water and chicken broth to a boil. Add the grits and butter, season with salt and pepper as desired, and stir to combine.

2. Cover, reduce the heat to medium, and cook, stirring occasionally, until thickened, about 10 minutes. Once the grits begin to soak up the liquid, stir in the brown sugar and garlic powder.

3. When the grits are done, stir in the coconut milk and smoked Gouda cheese. Season with salt as desired.

Cajun Seasoning

MAKES ABOUT ¼ CUP

2 tablespoons light brown sugar
1 tablespoon garlic powder
2 teaspoons onion powder
1 teaspoon dried oregano

1 teaspoon cracked black pepper
½ teaspoon kosher salt
¼ teaspoon crushed red pepper

1. Mix all the spices together in a small bowl. Store in an airtight container until ready to use.

Southern Inspired

Shrimp and Sausage Étouffée | SERVES 4

THE FRENCH WORD *étouffée* translates as "smothered," but when Southerners use the word, they're talking about one of the most exquisite representations of Southern cooking you'll find. This true Louisiana gem is a slow-cooked stew of shrimp, sausage, tomatoes, garlic, onions, peppers, celery, and Cajun spices, poured over a bed of rice. (The combo of onion, green bell pepper, and celery is referred to as the "holy trinity" in Cajun cooking.) Étouffée paired with a dry Riesling, Pinot Gris, or Chardonnay will be sure to leave a lasting impression.

¼ cup vegetable oil
1 small white onion, small diced
1 shallot, sliced
1 small green bell pepper, small diced
1 small red bell pepper, small diced
3 celery stalks, medium diced
1 small bunch scallions, sliced, plus
    more for garnish
2 smoked sausage or Cajun sausage
    links, sliced
6 garlic cloves, roughly chopped
3 bay leaves

Kosher salt
Cracked black pepper
¼ cup all-purpose flour
3 cups chicken broth
2 teaspoons Cajun seasoning,
    homemade (page 20) or
    store-bought
2½ cups tomato sauce
1 pound jumbo shrimp, peeled and
    deveined
2 cups cooked white rice, for
    serving

1. Heat the oil in a large Dutch oven or heavy-bottomed pot over medium-high heat. Add the onion and shallot and cook, stirring often, until brown, 4–5 minutes. If they do start to burn, reduce the heat to medium.

2. Add the bell peppers and celery and stir. (This will complete the trinity.) Cook for another 1–2 minutes to soften slightly, then add the scallions and cook until all the vegetables are browned.

3. Add the sausage, garlic, and bay leaves and stir to make sure the trinity is combined with the sausage. Season with salt and pepper to your taste.

(continued)

4. Once the sausage is nearly cooked, stir the flour into the mixture and cook, while continuing to stir, until a roux forms. You want to make sure the raw flour taste cooks out. The longer you cook the roux, the darker and richer it will become; for this recipe you want to cook the roux until it is a dark chocolaty brown.

5. Pour in the chicken broth and stir well to get rid of any lumps. Add the Cajun seasoning and tomato sauce and continue to stir. Bring the mixture up to a simmer and adjust the flavor with more salt or pepper.

6. Add the shrimp. Cover the pot and cook until the shrimp are cooked through, another couple of minutes. Remove the bay leaves.

7. Serve the étouffée over white rice and garnish with scallions.

Southern Sweet Tea–Brined Fried Chicken | SERVES 4–6

THIS IS BY FAR ONE OF MY FAVORITE RECIPES! Believe it or not, the origins of fried chicken have been attributed to Scottish settlers who emigrated to Southern colonies in the 1700s. But it was enslaved African cooks who enhanced these recipes with spices and frying techniques unique to their West African ancestry, turning this dish into a quintessential American classic with Southern roots. The addition of sweet tea—another Southern staple—used as a brine will add flavor and, above all else, juiciness. If you want to perform a magic trick at your next party or Sunday dinner, prepare this dish and watch it disappear before your very eyes!

1 (5-pound) chicken, cut into
    8 serving pieces

Sweet Tea Brine
2 quarts your favorite sweet tea
¼ cup kosher salt
5 sprigs fresh thyme
5 sprigs fresh rosemary
5 sprigs fresh basil (optional)

For Breading and Frying
2 cups whole milk
½ cup your favorite hot sauce, plus
    more for serving

½ cup smoked paprika, divided
½ cup Cajun seasoning, homemade
    (page 20) or store-bought,
    divided
4 cups all-purpose flour
2 tablespoons dried rosemary
1 tablespoon dried thyme
1 tablespoon crushed red pepper
1 tablespoon garlic powder
2 teaspoons onion powder
Vegetable oil, for frying
Sliced scallions, for garnish
    (optional)

1. Put the chicken pieces in a large pot and pour the sweet tea over them. The chicken pieces should be completely submerged; if not, add more tea. Add the salt and herb sprigs and cover the pot. Refrigerate for at least 2 hours or up to 24 hours.

(continued)

2. Remove the chicken pieces from the pot (discard the brining liquid) and put them in a large bowl. Pour the milk and hot sauce over them. Add ¼ cup of the smoked paprika and ¼ cup of the Cajun seasoning and turn the pieces over to evenly coat.

3. In another large bowl, whisk together the flour, remaining ¼ cup smoked paprika, remaining ¼ cup Cajun seasoning, dried rosemary, dried thyme, crushed red pepper, garlic powder, and onion powder.

4. Set a wire rack over a rimmed baking sheet. Working with one or two pieces at a time, remove the chicken from the milk mixture and dredge in the seasoned flour. Place the breaded chicken on the rack and allow to rest for 5–10 minutes.

5. In the meantime, pour vegetable oil into a large, heavy-bottomed pan or cast iron skillet to no more than halfway up the side. Prop or clip in a deep-fry thermometer so that the bulb is submerged in the oil. Heat over medium-high heat until the thermometer registers 350 degrees F. (Alternatively, you can use a deep fryer.)

6. Working in batches to not crowd the pan, gently submerge some of the chicken pieces in the hot oil. Fry for 7–10 minutes per side until the breading is golden brown and a thermometer inserted into the thickest part of the chicken reads 165 degrees F. Continue until all the chicken is fried.

7. Drizzle with additional hot sauce and garnish with sliced scallions, if you like.

Note: I recommend my signature Chef Jernard's Caribbean Island Fire Hot Wing Sauce, which brings sweet heat with peppers and pineapples. You can find it online, but feel free to use any hot sauce of your choice.

Crab-Stuffed Catfish
with Creole Sauce | SERVES 6–8

WHEN YOU HEAR THE TERM *RICH EATING,* what do you think of? For me growing up, it was when my parents stuffed our beloved Mississippi farm-raised catfish with sweet and tender crabmeat, topped it with a piquant Creole sauce, and served it with jambalaya, sautéed spinach, dirty rice, and love. You couldn't tell me we weren't rich!

---

8 tablespoons (1 stick) unsalted butter
½ cup small-diced yellow onion
2 small celery stalks, finely chopped
1 small bunch fresh flat-leaf parsley, minced, divided
8 ounces lump crabmeat

2 tablespoons Cajun seasoning, homemade (page 20) or store-bought
Juice of 1 small lemon
2 cups Italian bread crumbs, divided
2 tablespoons garlic powder
2 tablespoons onion powder
1 teaspoon smoked paprika
2 pounds catfish fillets, butterflied

---

1. Preheat the oven to 350 degrees F. Grease a rimmed baking sheet.

2. In a medium sauté pan or saucepan, melt the butter over medium-high heat. Add the onion and celery, cover, and sweat until soft and translucent, 2–3 minutes. (When sweating vegetables, the goal is to get the veggies soft, but you do not want to establish color.) Remove from the heat and stir in about three-quarters of the fresh parsley.

3. In a large bowl, combine the crabmeat, Cajun seasoning, lemon juice, and 1½ cups of the bread crumbs. Add the cooked onion mixture and mix with a fork to combine.

4. In a shallow bowl, mix the remaining ½ cup bread crumbs, garlic powder, onion powder, and smoked paprika.

5. Dip the butterflied catfish into the bread crumb mixture to coat both sides. Place about 1 tablespoon crab filling in the center of each breaded fillet. Start at one end of the fillet and carefully roll up to the other end. Place the fillets seam-side down on the prepared baking sheet.

Southern Inspired

6. Bake for 20–25 minutes, until the fish appears flaky. Top with Creole sauce (recipe follows) and garnish with the remaining fresh parsley.

Creole Sauce

3 tablespoons unsalted butter
2 Roma tomatoes, diced
½ cup chicken broth
Juice of 1 lemon
1 teaspoon minced fresh flat-leaf
   parsley

1 teaspoon Cajun seasoning,
   homemade (page 20) or
   store-bought
1 teaspoon sugar
Pinch crushed red pepper

1. Combine all the ingredients in a small saucepan and bring to a simmer over medium heat. Serve immediately, or let cool, then transfer to an airtight container and store in the refrigerator for up to 3 days. Rewarm gently to serve.

"Everything but Momma's Kitchen Sink" Meatloaf | SERVES 6–8

THIS RIGHT HERE IS FOR ALL the meatloaf fans out there! Even if you're not on "Team Meatloaf," have some faith in this inspired version of the American classic. My mom, Gwen, has a knack for weaving gold out of straw, and she outdid herself when she made her 24k meatloaf for us as kids. Gwen was ahead of the game; she fused together flavors from different cultures before fusion cuisine became a genre. For her meatloaf she used coconut milk, often used in Asian, Caribbean, and African cooking, added butter crackers instead of saltines, loaded it up with vegetables to get some nutrition into my vegetable-averse siblings, and blessed it with a sweet and spicy glaze to make this dish exceptional. I've kept many of those ingredients in this recipe but added canned chipotle peppers in adobo sauce and champagne vinegar to the glaze. If you don't have either of those on hand, smoked paprika and white wine vinegar will do just fine.

Meatloaf
1½ pounds 80% lean ground beef
½ cup diced yellow onion
½ cup diced green bell pepper
½ cup yellow corn kernels
½ cup sweet peas
1 cup crushed butter crackers
¼ cup coconut milk
2 large eggs
2 tablespoons ketchup
2 tablespoons Worcestershire sauce
2 teaspoons minced fresh flat-leaf parsley, plus more for garnish
1 teaspoon garlic powder
Kosher salt to taste
Ground white pepper to taste

Chipotle Brown Sugar Glaze
1 cup ketchup
½ cup canned chipotle peppers in adobo sauce (half chopped and half pureed)
3 tablespoons champagne vinegar
3 tablespoons light brown sugar

1. Preheat the oven to 375 degrees F. Grease a 9 × 5½-inch nonstick loaf pan with a light coating of cooking spray. Line the pan with a piece of parchment paper overhanging on two sides so it's easier to lift the meatloaf out when ready to serve.

2. In a large bowl, combine all the meatloaf ingredients. Mix with your hands or a spoon until thoroughly combined.

3. Press the meat mixture into the prepared loaf pan. Bake for 30 minutes.

4. In the meantime, combine the glaze ingredients in a small sauté pan and bring to a simmer over medium-high heat. Reduce the heat and simmer for 5 minutes.

5. Remove the meatloaf from the oven and brush about one-third of the glaze on top. Bake for another 25–30 minutes or until the center of the loaf registers 160–165 degrees F on a meat thermometer. Make sure not to let it dry out. Brush half of the remaining glaze on top.

6. Let the meatloaf rest in the pan for 10–15 minutes. This will allow it to keep its shape when ready to slice. Use the parchment as handles to remove the meatloaf from the pan. Garnish with parsley. Slice the meatloaf and serve with the remaining glaze on the side.

Creole Red Beans and Rice | SERVES 6-8

A TRUE CALLING CARD OF THE SOUTH, red beans and rice is a Louisiana staple. This dish was traditionally eaten on Mondays because that was typically "wash day," when women spent the day washing clothes by hand as they allowed a large pot of red beans, ham bones left over from Sunday dinner, fresh herbs, and spices to cook unattended as they worked. Served over a bed of rice, this dish has remained true to its roots, although substituting smoked or andouille sausage for the ham bone adds a nice kick of flavor. And feel free to eat this dish on Mondays, Tuesdays, Wednesdays . . . any day is a good day for Creole Red Beans and Rice.

---

1 pound dried red kidney beans *or* 2 (15.5-ounce) cans red kidney beans with liquid

2–6 cups low- or no-sodium chicken broth

¼ cup olive oil

1 medium yellow onion, small diced

1 green bell pepper, small diced

2 small celery stalks, small diced

2 tablespoons minced garlic

Kosher salt

Cracked black pepper

12–16 ounces chicken sausage, smoked sausage, or andouille sausage

1 teaspoon Cajun seasoning, homemade (page 20) or store-bought

1 teaspoon dried thyme

½ teaspoon cayenne pepper

¼ teaspoon dried sage

2 bay leaves

2 Roma tomatoes, small diced

1 tablespoon liquid smoke

Rice

4 cups low- or no-sodium chicken broth

2 cups long-grain white rice

Kosher salt

2 tablespoons minced fresh cilantro

Southern Inspired

1. If you are using dried beans, allow them to soak overnight in a large bowl of water. Drain the beans and transfer them to a medium pot. Pour 6 cups chicken broth over the beans and lightly simmer over medium heat until the beans are tender, 1–1½ hours. (Be careful not to overcook or the beans may break and become mushy.) If you're using canned beans for a shortcut, add the beans with their liquid to 2 cups simmering chicken broth and cook for about 10 minutes over medium heat.

2. When the beans are almost done, heat the oil in another large pot over medium-high heat. Add the onion, bell pepper, celery, and garlic and sauté until the onion is translucent and the pepper is soft, 3–4 minutes. Season with salt and pepper as desired. Transfer to a bowl.

3. In the same pot, cook the sausage until golden brown, about 5 minutes. Return the onion, pepper, celery, and garlic mixture to the pot and stir into the sausage. Then add the Cajun seasoning, thyme, cayenne, and sage and toast for about 1 minute.

4. Add the bay leaves, tomatoes, and liquid smoke. You can use more or less liquid smoke depending on how smoky you want the flavor to be. Remove from the heat and set aside until the beans are cooked, then pour the cooked beans into the sausage and vegetable mixture. Remove the bay leaves.

5. Meanwhile, make the rice. In a medium pot, bring the chicken broth to a boil over medium-high heat. Add the rice, season with salt as desired, cover, and cook over medium-low heat according to the package instructions until the rice is tender and the liquid has been absorbed. Mix the cilantro into the cooked rice and serve with the red beans.

CHAPTER 2
THE *Main* EVENT

WATCHING MY PARENTS COOK WAS LIKE TAKING RINGSIDE seats on fight night, only minus the fight. The energy that filled the air in anticipation of the meal being served was exhilarating. Friends and family came for the headliner, the showstopper dish—the main event! They didn't realize it at the time, but my parents used to host live cooking shows in their kitchen just about every Saturday evening. Saturdays were the days when neighbors would "just stop by," then somehow file into the kitchen, taking their seats as my mom chopped vegetables and prepped her ingredients before performing some culinary magic. Other neighbors would break off and follow my dad to the wood-burning fire pit out back as he placed his mac and cheese on the grill just so. It truly was "The Matt and Gwen Show"!

Now I don't know about you, but I've never met a person who didn't like mac and cheese—and I don't know what I'd do if I did. My dad blended his Southern roots with French and Italian elements to create his signature seafood mac and cheese. The smoothness and creaminess of his béchamel was always a source of pride, but once he added his smoked and Italian cheeses, coupled with lobster, shrimp, or crabmeat, the result was the tastiest mac and cheese with the greatest pull effect you've ever seen. Pull effect, you say? That's right, see for yourself when you serve a portion of my version of this masterpiece and watch those long, thick strands of cheese pull from dish to plate—like my dad used to say, "Watch that macaroni pull like pizza!" This is what you want!

Get ready, because in this chapter, I'm serving up nine dishes that will take center stage at your next dinner party or special date night—and they're sure to bring you a standing ovation, so you better start practicing those bows!

Smoky Seafood Mac and Cheese | SERVES 8–10

I'M CALLING ALL MY FELLOW CHEESE LOVERS—my *turophiles*—out there with this macaroni and cheese treasure. I may be speaking Greek, but this recipe is my take on an all-American classic. This dish right here is not for the faint of heart because I've packed it with smoked Gouda, smoked cheddar, and creamy Gruyère and brought some Southern heat with the addition of andouille sausage. If that wasn't enough, I've elevated it to a level of decadence that only lobster can provide.

---

1 pound elbow macaroni
1 cup sliced andouille sausage
8 tablespoons (1 stick) plus 2 tablespoons unsalted butter, divided
½ cup all-purpose flour
2 cups heavy cream
2 cups half-and-half
1 tablespoon smoked paprika
½ teaspoon ground nutmeg
Kosher salt
Cracked black pepper

3 cups shredded smoked Gouda cheese, divided
2 cups shredded smoked cheddar cheese, divided
1 cup shredded Gruyère cheese, divided
1½ pounds cooked lobster meat, diced into large chunks
¼ cup plain bread crumbs
1 (1½–2-pound) whole lobster, steamed (optional; see note)

---

1. Preheat the oven to 350 degrees F. Have ready a 9 × 13-inch casserole dish.

2. Bring a large pot of salted water to a boil. Add the pasta and cook according to the package directions until al dente. Drain and set aside.

3. Meanwhile, in a deep pot or large Dutch oven, sauté the andouille sausage over medium-high heat for 5 minutes or until golden brown. Add the stick of butter and allow it to melt. Add the flour and cook for 3–5 minutes, stirring constantly, to fully incorporate the flour into the butter (be careful not to let the flour burn). Add the heavy cream and half-and-half and stir until the sauce begins to thicken. Season with the smoked paprika, nutmeg, and salt and pepper to taste.

(continued)

4. Reserve ¼ cup each of the Gouda, cheddar, and Gruyère cheeses, and fold the remaining cheeses into the mixture. Stir to combine. Stir in the cooked lobster.

5. Pour the mac and cheese into the prepared casserole dish. Sprinkle the reserved ¾ cup cheese on top.

6. Melt the remaining 2 tablespoons butter in a medium sauté pan over medium heat. Add the bread crumbs and sauté until lightly golden. Sprinkle on top of the mac and cheese.

7. Bake for about 30 minutes or until golden brown and bubbly.

Note: It's entirely optional, but to really bring down the house, you can bake the mac and cheese with a whole steamed lobster sticking out of the top, as shown. When serving, crack open the whole lobster and pass the extra meat around the table.

Southern Inspired

My Dad's Oxtails

with Momma's Buttery Garlic Whipped Potatoes | **SERVES 4–6**

DESPITE THE HARDSHIPS AND CHALLENGES I've had to overcome throughout my life, I've received many blessings along the way. For starters, I had the good fortune of being raised in a very loving and supportive family. As a child, watching my parents cook together was truly the epitome of love. Hearing blues play as I watched my dad season his oxtails, getting them ready for the pressure cooker as my mom, by his side, would laugh and playfully tease him in between peeling, boiling, and whipping those buttery potatoes into perfect pillowy fluffiness—this is a memory that I carry with me every day.

---

3 tablespoons olive oil

3 medium russet potatoes, large diced

2 large carrots, large diced

1 medium yellow onion, medium diced

10 garlic cloves, roughly chopped

Kosher salt

Cracked black pepper

6 pounds oxtails

1½ cups all-purpose flour

1–1½ cups chicken or beef broth

¼ cup balsamic vinegar

¼ cup Worcestershire sauce

¼ cup browning sauce

3 tablespoons tomato paste

2 bay leaves

2 teaspoons ground allspice

1 teaspoon garlic powder

1 teaspoon onion powder

¼ teaspoon dried oregano

¼ teaspoon dried thyme

1 whole Scotch bonnet or habanero pepper (optional)

---

1. Set a pressure cooker to sauté and pour in the oil. Once it's hot, add the potatoes, carrots, onion, and garlic and cook until the onion is translucent, about 5 minutes. Season with salt and pepper as desired. Transfer the vegetables to a bowl.

2. In a large bowl, toss the oxtails in the flour and tap off the excess flour. The flour will add texture to the meat and thicken the gravy.

3. Add more oil to the pressure cooker if needed and sear the oxtails until they are golden on each side.

(continued)

4. Return the vegetables to the pressure cooker, along with the remaining ingredients. Stir everything well.

5. Bring the mixture up to a simmer and close the lid. Make sure to seal the vent knob. Turn the pressure cooker function to high and set the timer for 40 minutes.

6. While the oxtails are cooking, prepare the potatoes (recipe follows).

7. When the timer goes off, carefully release the venting knob on the pressure cooker so the steam can escape. Remove the bay leaves.

8. Serve the oxtails and vegetables with their sauce, with the whipped potatoes alongside.

Momma's Buttery Garlic Whipped Potatoes

6–10 large Yukon Gold potatoes, peeled and large diced
Kosher salt
8 tablespoons (1 stick) unsalted butter
2 tablespoons minced garlic
¼ cup garlic powder
2 tablespoons onion powder
½ cup heavy cream
¼ cup sour cream
¼ cup chicken broth
Ground white pepper
Minced fresh chives, for garnish

1. Put the potatoes in a large pot and cover with water. Add 1 tablespoon salt. Bring to a boil over high heat, then lower the heat to a simmer and cook the potatoes until they're fork-tender, 10–15 minutes. Drain the potatoes and transfer to a large bowl.

2. Melt the butter in a medium sauté pan over medium-high heat. Add the garlic and sweat until soft, about 3 minutes. Add the garlic powder, onion powder, heavy cream, sour cream, and chicken broth and bring to a light simmer for 5 minutes.

3. Pour the creamy liquid over the cooked potatoes and carefully use a whisk to whip the potatoes until there are no lumps.

4. Season with salt and white pepper as desired. Garnish with chives.

Southern Inspired

Deep-Fried Snow Crab Legs | SERVES 4-6

THIS DISH IS LIKE CHRISTMAS, Thanksgiving, and my birthday rolled into one. It's the ultimate celebration of indulgence that stems from my childhood and brings back beautiful memories of family gatherings. From the deep cold waters of the North Atlantic and Pacific oceans to the warm tables of the deep South, my Deep-Fried Snow Crab Legs blend North and South in a jubilee of crispy on the outside, succulent on the inside—and topped with a zesty sauce, just to keep it interesting.

8 cups water

2 cups chicken broth

¼ cup Old Bay seasoning

4 bay leaves

2 medium lemons, halved, plus additional lemon wedges for serving

10 snow crab legs

Chopped fresh flat-leaf parsley or cilantro, for garnish

Crab Sauce

1½ cups your favorite hot sauce

4 tablespoons (½ stick) unsalted butter

Juice of 1 medium lemon

¼ cup minced garlic

2 tablespoons light brown sugar

1 tablespoon chili powder

1 teaspoon chili flakes

For Battering and Frying

1½ cups all-purpose flour

¾ cup cornstarch

1 tablespoon baking powder

1 tablespoon lemon pepper seasoning (I like Chef Jernard's Parmesan Lemon Pepper Ranch Seasoning)

10 ounces sparkling water, or more as needed

Vegetable oil, for frying

1. In a large pot, combine the water, chicken broth, Old Bay, bay leaves, and lemon halves. Bring to a boil over high heat. Add the crab legs and cook until they turn bright pink, no more than 10 minutes. Remove from the heat and take the crab legs out of the broth to cool for about 10 minutes.

2. Meanwhile, make the crab sauce. Combine the hot sauce, butter, lemon juice, garlic, brown sugar, chili powder, and chili flakes in a small saucepan over medium heat. Bring the mixture to a simmer. Once it starts to thicken, turn off the heat.

Southern Inspired

3. Break the crabmeat from the shells using your hands or scissors. (Scissors make for better cuts.)

4. In a medium bowl, combine the flour, cornstarch, baking powder, and lemon pepper seasoning. Blend with a fork, then add the sparkling water little by little to make a thin batter.

5. Pour the vegetable oil into a large, heavy-bottomed pot or Dutch oven to no more than halfway up the side. Prop or clip in a deep-fry thermometer so that the bulb is submerged in the oil. Heat the oil over medium-high heat until the thermometer registers 375 degrees F. (Alternatively, you can use a deep fryer.)

6. Dip each crab leg in the batter, then gently lay it in the hot oil. Fry the crab legs until golden brown, 6–8 minutes.

7. Serve the crab legs garnished with parsley, with the crab sauce and lemon wedges on the side.

Blackened Salmon with Coconut Cream Crawfish Sauce | SERVES 4

CALL THEM WHAT YOU LIKE: crayfish, crawdads, mudbugs, or freshwater lobsters. But where I'm from, they're called crawfish—and will always be crawfish. No matter what you choose to call this unbelievably tasty and versatile crustacean, there's no denying that these shrimp cousins are a quintessential part of Southern cuisine. I've based this recipe on my family's tradition of finding new ways to blend our familiar standbys with unexpected ingredients to create exceptional dishes. Here, I've called upon coconut milk to add its creaminess and hint of sweet to balance the spicy kick of the blackened salmon. A feast for the eyes and a treat for your table!

Blackening Seasoning

1½ teaspoons Cajun seasoning, homemade (page 20) or store-bought

1½ teaspoons cayenne pepper

1½ teaspoons chili powder

1½ teaspoons smoked paprika

Salmon

1 pound crawfish tails or large shrimp, peeled and deveined

4 (6-ounce) salmon fillets, skinned if desired

2 tablespoons honey

8 tablespoons (1 stick) unsalted butter, divided

1 tablespoon olive oil

3 garlic cloves, roughly chopped

1 green bell pepper, diced

4 celery stalks, diced

1 yellow onion, diced

1 cup diced Roma tomato

1 cup coconut milk

Kosher salt

2 cups cooked wild rice or wild rice blend, for serving

1. In a small bowl, stir together all the blackening seasoning ingredients.

2. In a large bowl, sprinkle a little bit of the blackening seasoning over the crawfish tails and toss to coat.

3. Drizzle the salmon with honey on both sides and sprinkle half of the remaining blackening seasoning over each side of the fillets. The honey will allow the seasoning to stick.

Southern Inspired

4. Melt 3 tablespoons of the butter with the olive oil in a large skillet or grill pan over medium-high heat. Place the salmon fillets in the pan (skin-side down if your fillets have skin on) and cook for about 4 minutes on each side for medium-rare/medium, or to your preferred doneness.

5. While the salmon cooks, melt the remaining 5 tablespoons butter in a medium sauté pan over medium-high heat. Stir in the garlic and trinity of bell pepper, celery, and onion and cook until tender, about 2 minutes. Add the crawfish, lower the heat to medium, and stir to combine. Cover and cook for a few minutes, until the crawfish are cooked through and tender.

6. Add the diced tomato, coconut milk, and remaining blackening seasoning. Cook for a few minutes more, until the sauce comes to a simmer.

7. Divide the wild rice onto four plates. Place a salmon fillet on top of the wild rice and serve topped with the coconut cream crawfish sauce.

Rosemary and Mint Lamb Chops
with Maple and Balsamic Brussels Sprouts | SERVES 4

YOU MIGHT BE SAYING, "Chef, you had me at lamb chops, but you lost me with Brussels sprouts." I get it, but you haven't tried *these* Brussels sprouts. This cabbage cousin, usually served at Thanksgiving—often overboiled, underseasoned, and left by its lonesome on the dinner plate—transcends its bitter persona to take this dish to an unexpected level of sophistication and delight. Thinly sliced Brussels sprouts lovingly sautéed with butter and bacon and topped with a sweet maple and balsamic glaze—paired with my rosemary and mint lamb chops, seared to perfection. This dish may very well top your date night rotation.

2 tablespoons avocado oil	3–4 tablespoons chopped fresh
10–12 lamb rib chops	mint, plus some whole sprigs or
1 tablespoon minced garlic	leaves for garnish
Kosher salt	3 tablespoons chopped fresh
Cracked black pepper	rosemary
2 tablespoons unsalted butter	3 tablespoons chopped fresh flat-
	leaf parsley
	2 tablespoons chopped fresh thyme

1. Heat the oil in a large cast iron skillet over medium-high heat. Season the lamb chops on both sides with the garlic, salt, and black pepper to taste.

2. Sear the lamb chops on one side for 3 minutes, then flip and sear on the other side for 3 minutes for medium. (If you prefer them medium-well, cook for an additional 2–3 minutes per side.)

3. Add the butter and chopped herbs to the pan. Spoon the butter mixture over the lamb chops for roughly 1 minute while they cook.

4. Remove the skillet from heat and allow the chops to rest for about 5 minutes. Garnish with the mint leaves or sprigs and serve with the Brussels sprouts (recipe follows).

2 tablespoons unsalted butter

4 strips pork or turkey bacon, cut into ¼–½-inch pieces

1 shallot, roughly chopped

1 teaspoon minced garlic

1 pound Brussels sprouts, trimmed and thinly sliced

2 tablespoons avocado oil

Kosher salt

Cracked black pepper

¼ cup plus 2 tablespoons maple syrup, divided

2 tablespoons balsamic vinegar

1. Melt the butter in a cast iron skillet over medium-high heat. Add the bacon and cook for 5 minutes to render the fat. Add the shallot and garlic and sauté until golden brown, another 2–3 minutes.

2. Add the Brussels sprouts and avocado oil and season with salt and pepper as desired. Cook for 4–5 minutes, stirring occasionally. Add ¼ cup of the maple syrup and the balsamic vinegar. Reduce the heat to medium and sauté for another few minutes to coat evenly.

3. Transfer the mixture to a serving dish and drizzle with the remaining 2 tablespoons maple syrup. Season with more salt and pepper to taste.

Southern Inspired

Jernard's General Tso's Chicken | SERVES 4–6

MY CHILDREN AND I LOVE MAKING THIS DISH together. Maybe they enjoy the cornstarch batter sticking to their fingers (it doesn't have to, but you know—kids), or tossing the crispy bite-size fried chicken pieces in the sweet and sticky sauce made of rice wine vinegar, brown sugar, hoisin sauce, garlic, crushed red pepper, and spices. But I'd like to think they enjoy the time we spend making it together as much as I do. Why order out when you can whip up this classic—Chef Jernard style?

Vegetable oil, for frying
6 boneless, skinless chicken thighs
3 teaspoons garlic powder, divided
3 teaspoons onion powder, divided
Kosher salt
Cracked black pepper
2 cups all-purpose flour
½ cup cornstarch
¾ to 1 cup cold water, or more as
  needed
Toasted sesame seeds, for garnish
3 cups cooked sticky rice, for
  serving

Sliced scallions, for garnish

General Tso Sauce
½ cup loosely packed light brown
  sugar
½ cup hoisin sauce
⅓ cup soy sauce
2 tablespoons rice wine vinegar
2 teaspoons toasted sesame oil
1 garlic clove, minced
Pinch crushed red pepper

1. Pour vegetable oil into a wok or large, heavy-bottomed pot no more than halfway up the side. Prop or clip in a deep-fry thermometer so that the bulb is submerged in the oil. Heat over medium-low heat until the thermometer registers 350 degrees F. Set a wire rack in a rimmed baking sheet.

2. While the oil is heating, on a plastic cutting board, cut the chicken thighs into large chunks and place them in a large bowl. Season the chicken pieces with 1 teaspoon of the garlic powder, 1 teaspoon of the onion powder, and salt and pepper as desired. Toss to coat.

(continued)

3. In another large bowl, whisk together the flour, cornstarch, remaining 2 teaspoons garlic powder, remaining 2 teaspoons onion powder, and salt and pepper as desired. If you want a softer, less crunchy coating on your chicken, you can mix 1 cup flour, 1 cup cornstarch, and 1½ cups water. Add the chicken and toss to thoroughly coat in the flour mixture, pouring in the cold water as you do. This will help the batter stick to the chicken to create a delicious, crispy coating when it's fried. If it's still too thick, add more water, a tablespoon at a time, until it reaches the consistency of a thick pancake batter.

4. Working in batches, fry the chicken until golden brown and transfer to the rack.

5. Pour off the oil and wipe out the wok. Combine all the sauce ingredients in the wok and bring to a boil over high heat.

6. Add the fried chicken and toss to combine.

7. Sprinkle with toasted sesame seeds and serve over sticky rice, garnished with scallions.

Southern Inspired

"Chef of Love's" Shrimp Scampi | SERVES 4–6

SOME MIGHT ASK WHY a shrimp scampi recipe belongs in a cookbook of Southern-inspired dishes. For me, the answer is clear. I have a deep appreciation for global cuisines, and I find great joy in developing new flavor profiles based on my meaningful Southern upbringing. Sometimes you must turn a recipe on its head and reinterpret it into something new, but occasionally you need to stay true to the original while making a simple yet impactful change that makes the dish extraordinary. Here, I've made a traditional shrimp scampi but blessed it with diced bacon as a finishing touch. If you want to turn up the Southern charm, try hickory-smoked slab bacon, but any bacon will add the right amount of smokiness to this favorite.

---

6 tablespoons olive oil, divided
Kosher salt
1 pound spaghetti
6 tablespoons unsalted butter
Cracked black pepper
2–3 tablespoons minced garlic

1 pound jumbo shrimp, peeled and deveined
1½ tablespoons garlic powder
1 cup dry white wine
1 cup chopped cooked bacon
½–1 cup roughly chopped fresh flat-leaf parsley

---

1. Bring a large pot of water to a boil. Add 3 tablespoons of the olive oil and generously season with salt. Add the spaghetti and cook according to the package directions until al dente, stirring once in a while to make sure the pasta doesn't stick together.

2. While the pasta cooks, start on your scampi sauce. Melt the butter with the remaining 3 tablespoons olive oil in a large sauté pan over medium-high heat. Add the minced garlic and cook, stirring, until aromatic, 1–2 minutes. Do not let the garlic burn!

(continued)

3. Add your shrimp, season with salt and pepper, and sprinkle with garlic powder. Stir the shrimp to coat with the seasonings and cook for about 1 minute on each side or until the shrimp are opaque.

4. Add the white wine and cook until the wine reduces by almost half, 4–5 minutes.

5. Once the pasta is cooked, add it right from the pasta water using tongs, then sprinkle on the cooked bacon pieces and parsley. Toss everything to combine and serve right away.

Southern Inspired

Black and Pink Peppercorn–Crusted Petite Filet with Whiskey Glaze

and Decadent Creamed Spinach | **SERVES 4**

TO MANY, THE FIRST TIME preparing a steak dinner feels more like a rite of passage rather than simply making a meal. Learning about the different cuts, managing cooking times, and mastering spice blends feels very grown-up, even a little intimidating. But with this dish, you can rest assured that I've got you covered! Not only is this recipe easy to master, but it's equal parts impressive and flavorful with its snappy whiskey glaze. Pair it with creamed spinach and you've got a "sure shot" in your bag of tricks. Time to take your seat at the grown-ups' table!

½ cup mixed pink and black peppercorns

4 (4-ounce) petite filets

Kosher salt

¼ cup olive oil

6 large garlic cloves, divided

4 tablespoons (½ stick) unsalted butter, divided

3 sprigs fresh thyme

3 sprigs fresh rosemary

¼ cup light brown sugar

½–¾ cup Tennessee whiskey

1. Pour the peppercorns into a large bowl. With your fingertips, press down on the peppercorns to break up the pink ones a little. Press the steaks into the peppercorns so they are coated in them and season with salt.

2. Heat the olive oil in a large cast iron skillet over medium-high heat until the oil starts to smoke slightly.

3. Roughly chop 3 of the garlic cloves and add them to the hot oil. After a few seconds, the garlic should start to brown. Carefully place the steaks in the pan—some of the peppercorns will fall off, but try not to lose too many. Sear for 2–3 minutes on one side, then flip them over and sear for roughly the same time on the other side. (While the steaks are searing, you can start your creamed spinach; recipe follows.)

4. Add 2 tablespoons of the butter, the thyme, rosemary, and remaining 3 garlic cloves (whole but peeled) to the pan and continue searing the steak until golden brown on the other side.

(continued)

5. Carefully tilt the pan (wrap a towel around the handle if needed) to gather the sauce at one corner. With a large spoon, baste each steak with the hot, bubbly butter. Cook until the desired internal temperature is reached: 130–135 degrees F for medium-rare, 135–145 degrees F for medium, or 155–160 degrees F for well-done.

6. Transfer the steaks, herbs, and garlic to a plate and let rest for 5 minutes.

7. Meanwhile, in the same pan, melt the remaining 2 tablespoons butter over medium-high to high heat, making sure not to let it burn.

8. Add the brown sugar and stir to dissolve into the butter. Carefully pour in the whiskey and stir to combine. The sauce should start bubbling; lower the heat to medium and simmer to let the sauce reduce for 2–3 minutes. You will know when the sauce is ready when it appears thick and glossy.

9. Lay the steaks on a serving platter and pour some of the whiskey glaze over the top. Serve with creamed spinach (recipe follows) and extra glaze on the side.

Decadent Creamed Spinach

4 tablespoons (½ stick) unsalted butter	**1 teaspoon garlic powder**
1 shallot, thinly sliced	**1 pound baby spinach**
6 garlic cloves, roughly chopped	**¼ cup grated Parmesan cheese**
1–2 tablespoons all-purpose flour	**Kosher salt**
1½–2 cups heavy cream	**Cracked black pepper**

1. Melt the butter in a medium skillet over medium-high heat. Add the shallot and garlic and stir. As the aromatics begin to brown, add the flour and stir to allow the flour and butter to cook together to make a roux. Continue to stir as the roux cooks for a few more seconds.

2. Whisk in the heavy cream until smooth. Bring the sauce up to a gentle simmer.

3. Add the garlic powder and spinach and press the leaves down into the creamy sauce. Allow the spinach to wilt, stirring occasionally, for about 1 minute. Cover and continue to cook for 6–7 minutes over medium heat.

4. Stir in the Parmesan cheese, salt as desired, and top with a sprinkle of cracked black pepper.

Southern Inspired

Crispy Honey Shrimp over Garlic Rice Noodles | SERVES 4

HATS OFF TO MY LATE DAD, MATT, for introducing my palate to Chinese, Thai, Japanese, and Korean food. On our road trips back to Mississippi from Chicago, where I'm originally from, he always made it a point to stop at various Asian restaurants along the way to open our minds and taste buds to different cultures and cuisines. The memories of those trips left such an impression that I became classically trained in Asian cooking and cofounded an Asian fusion restaurant at one point. And what better way to honor my dad than by sharing this perfectly balanced dish with you. The crispiness of the shrimp, complemented by the perfect kiss of honey and served over garlic noodles, is only enhanced by the fragrant smell and flavor of sesame oil. Perfection!

---

2 cups cornstarch
1–1½ cups water
Vegetable oil, for frying
1 pound large shrimp, peeled (tails left on) and deveined
Kosher salt
Cracked black pepper
1 tablespoon avocado oil
¼ cup minced garlic
1 cup low-sodium soy sauce
2 tablespoons honey
2 tablespoons light brown sugar
1 tablespoon hoisin sauce

1 teaspoon toasted sesame oil
1 inch ginger, minced
1 cup canned sliced water chestnuts, drained
1 cup snow peas
2 medium carrots, sliced into thin medallions
3 scallions, sliced
1 pound rice vermicelli noodles, cooked
Chopped fresh flat-leaf parsley, for garnish (optional)

---

1. In a small bowl, whisk together the cornstarch and 1 cup of the water until it has the consistency of a thin batter. Add up to ½ cup more water if needed.

2. Pour vegetable oil into a large, heavy bottom pot or Dutch oven to no more than halfway up the side. Prop or clip in a deep-fry thermometer so that the bulb is submerged in the oil. Heat the oil over medium-high heat until the thermometer registers 350 degrees F. (Alternatively, you can use a deep fryer.) Line a plate with paper towels.

3. Working in batches, dip the shrimp into the cornstarch mixture, then place in the oil and fry until golden and crispy, 3–4 minutes. Transfer to the paper towels to drain. Sprinkle the shrimp with salt and pepper to your taste.

4. Heat the avocado oil in a large wok or nonstick skillet over high heat. Add the garlic and cook, stirring constantly, until it is lightly golden brown.

5. Add the soy sauce, honey, brown sugar, hoisin sauce, sesame oil, and ginger and mix to combine in the pan. Bring the mixture to a boil and continue to cook until it reduces to a thick glaze, about 1 minute or less (this happens fast!).

6. Toss the shrimp into the sauce and turn to coat evenly. Transfer the glazed shrimp to a plate, leaving the remaining sauce in the wok.

7. Toss the water chestnuts, snow peas, carrots, scallions, and rice noodles in the sauce. I prefer to use special wok spoons because they allow you to stir and scoop at the same time, but if you don't have them, tongs are fine.

8. Plate the veggies and noodles with the shrimp on top. Garnish with parsley if desired.

CHAPTER 3

NOTHING BUT
Bites

$\mathcal{M}$Y BEAUTIFUL WIFE, KEENA, AND I MET IN COLLEGE. FOR our first date I knew I had to impress her, so I took a page from my dad's playbook and cooked for her! (That's right, my dad used to woo my mom with his moves both in and out of the kitchen— did I mention I'm one of 11 kids?!) He made his signature appetizer "bite" with a bed of pineapple pico de gallo and lovingly placed the shrimp on top, serving it in a glass dish. But for Keena, I knew I had to do even better. I decided I was going to sway her by turning up the heat with Creole seasoning and serving it in a fancy martini glass! I called it the Skinny Dippin' Shrimp Cocktail—as you can tell from the name, it was a dish d'amour. And it worked, because 23 years and 9 nine kids later, here we are! (They don't call me the Chef of Love for nothing.) I promised Keena that I'd always keep that dish special for us, so when I put it on my menu, I tweaked the recipe a bit and renamed it Creole Pineapple Shrimp Martini. It has remained my most requested menu item for the past 15 years.

But there's more: I got a secret to tell.

Earlier in my career as a chef, celebrities would hire me to secretly cook romantic meals for their date nights. That's right, I was the "Hitch" chef for the romantically inclined yet culinarily challenged! I used to prep and cook meals in clients' homes, help set the mood for the night, and then sneak out the back door before their dates arrived. My Creole Pineapple Shrimp Martini was always first on the menu and it worked every time.

Problem was, it worked so well that my would-be chefs had to keep up the charade for date number two. I can't tell you how many calls I'd get from nervous clients telling me how much their dates loved the food, but now they didn't know what to do since the bar had been set so high. I knew *exactly* what they needed to do—keep paying me to cook or pay me to teach *them* how to cook. Man, I did that for a long time—even set up my kids' college fund with that one!

Let me help you set the mood or get the party started with these seven recipes for tantalizing savory bites, including Lollipop Drumsticks with Whiskey Chipotle Sauce, Smoky Charbroiled Oysters, and, of course, that shrimp cocktail. You never know where things may lead!

Creole Pineapple Shrimp Martini | SERVES 4

IF YOU WANT TO SERVE A DISH that your guests will eat with their eyes before gracing their lips, this is it. In less than 15 minutes, you can prepare this stunning appetizer that will captivate your guests with its sweet and peppery aroma, courtesy of coating extra-large shrimp with silky barbecue sauce, smoked paprika, bell peppers, onions, and garlic—alongside the guest of honor, sweet and juicy diced pineapple. The wow-factor is off the charts; it's pointless to resist!

Olive oil
4 garlic cloves, roughly chopped
½ yellow bell pepper, medium diced
1 small yellow onion, small diced
12 extra-large shrimp, peeled (tails left on) and deveined
1½ tablespoons light brown sugar
¾–1 cup tomato sauce

1 teaspoon smoked paprika
Kosher salt
Cracked black pepper
⅓ cup your favorite barbecue sauce
1 cup small-diced pineapple
Minced fresh flat-leaf parsley, for garnish

---

1. In a medium sauté pan over medium-high heat, heat just enough olive oil to coat the pan.

2. Add the garlic and bell pepper and cook until the garlic is nice and toasted and the pepper turns a bit golden in color. Stir in the onion and cook until translucent, 1–2 minutes.

3. Place the shrimp on top of the vegetables. Sprinkle the brown sugar on the shrimp, followed by the tomato sauce and smoked paprika. Season with salt and pepper as desired.

4. Pour in the barbecue sauce and stir everything to combine. Simmer for 2–3 minutes to reduce the sauce. The shrimp should be tender and not overcooked.

5. Have ready four martini glasses. Spoon the sauce into the center of each martini glass about a third of the way up. Add a few chunks of pineapple and then line the rim with three shrimp. Sprinkle with fresh parsley and serve!

Southern Inspired

Lollipop Drumsticks with Whiskey Chipotle Sauce | SERVES 6-8

THE PREP FOR THIS DISH is a bit more involved than most of my other "bites" in this chapter, but I promise it'll be worth it when you serve these party-starters. The lollipop appearance of these little treasures will only endear them more to your guests as they enjoy bites smothered in a rich, sweet, and smoky glaze compliments of chipotle peppers, brown sugar, and whiskey. If you're in a rush, you can cut down on time by skipping the "lollipop" prep of the chicken, but I urge you to try it at least once.

---

12 chicken drumsticks
¼ cup plus 2 tablespoons light brown sugar
2 tablespoons garlic powder
2 tablespoons smoked paprika
2 tablespoons onion powder
2 teaspoons dried oregano
Kosher salt
Cracked black pepper
2½ tablespoons canned chipotles in adobo sauce, pureed
2½ tablespoons Worcestershire sauce
3–4 tablespoons Tennessee whiskey
Fresh parsley, for garnish (optional)

Whiskey Chipotle Sauce
¼ cup light brown sugar
1¼ teaspoons onion powder
1¼ teaspoons garlic powder
3 tablespoons unsalted butter
1 cup canned chipotles in adobo sauce, pureed
¾–1 cup Tennessee whiskey
3–4 tablespoons Worcestershire sauce
Kosher salt to taste
Cracked black pepper to taste

---

1. Preheat the oven to 400 degrees F. Have ready a greased or nonstick 12-cup muffin tin.

2. To shape each chicken leg like a lollipop, first use a small, sharp knife or kitchen shears to cut and remove the skin that covers the bone around the knuckle, then cut the tendon. Use the back of your knife or hands to push the skin down toward the meat. Remove the knuckle cap and discard.

Southern Inspired

3. In a small bowl, combine the brown sugar, garlic powder, smoked paprika, onion powder, oregano, and salt and pepper as desired. Add the chipotles in adobo, Worcestershire, and whiskey and mix well to combine.

4. Dip each chicken lollipop into the sauce mixture and coat evenly.

5. Place the lollipops in the muffin tin with their legs pointing upright. Wrap aluminum foil around the exposed bone ends to keep them from turning too dark in the oven.

6. Roast for about 40 minutes or until the internal temperature reaches 165 degrees F.

7. Toward the end of the cooking time, in a small saucepan, combine all the whiskey chipotle sauce ingredients. Cook over medium-high heat, stirring occasionally, for about 10 minutes.

8. Dip the cooked lollipops in the sauce and serve garnished with parsley if you like.

Red, White, and Blue BBQ Nachos | SERVES 6–8

SERVE THIS CROWD PLEASER for the Fourth of July, a tailgate party, or your next binge-watching self-care weekend—because it will not disappoint the nacho lover in you. Red, for the slow-cooked pulled beef smothered lovingly in piquant spices and barbecue sauce. White, for the aged white cheddar cheese sauce that makes this dish irresistible. And blue, for the blue corn chips that add beautiful color and the right amount of crunch to each bite!

¼ cup smoked paprika
¼ cup onion powder
¼ cup garlic powder
¼ cup dry mustard
¼ cup light brown sugar
Kosher salt
Cracked black pepper
1 (2-pound) beef top round roast
1 quart beef stock
1 tablespoon liquid smoke
1 cup your favorite barbecue sauce,
     plus more for serving

Cheese Sauce
8 tablespoons (1 stick) unsalted
     butter
½ cup all-purpose flour
2 cups whole milk
2 cups shredded aged white cheddar
     cheese
Kosher salt
Cracked black pepper

Nachos
2 (8-ounce) bags blue and white corn
     tortilla chips
Sliced scallions
1 jalapeño, thinly sliced

---

1. Preheat the oven to 375 degrees F.

2. In a small bowl, combine the smoked paprika, onion powder, garlic powder, dry mustard, brown sugar, and salt and pepper as desired.

3. Rub the spice mixture all over the beef roast, massaging it into the meat. Use just enough to coat the beef; you can keep any extra dry rub in an airtight container for later use. It will keep for a few months.

(continued)

4. Pour the beef stock and liquid smoke into a Dutch oven. Carefully place your seasoned roast in the pot. Cover and roast for 1–1½ hours or until the meat is fork-tender and beginning to fall apart.

5. Shred the cooked meat with two forks and stir in the barbecue sauce.

6. To make the cheese sauce, melt the butter in a medium saucepan over medium-high heat. Add the flour and cook, whisking constantly, until a blond roux forms, 2–3 minutes. Whisk in the milk in a slow stream to avoid lumps. Bring the sauce to a light simmer, then whisk in the cheese and stir until melted and stringy. Remove from the heat and season with salt and pepper as desired.

7. Build the nachos! Layer the chips with the shredded top round meat. Pour the cheese sauce over the top. Garnish with scallions and sliced jalapeños and drizzle with more barbecue sauce. Enjoy right away!

Southern Inspired

Smoky Charbroiled Oysters | SERVES 4

OYSTERS ARE ONE OF THOSE DELICACIES that may cause a moment of hesitancy when seen on a menu or at your local fish market, but please don't let its mystery stop you from enjoying this succulent and versatile ingredient. My Smoky Charbroiled Oysters may just be your gateway to enjoying their charm. Shucked and grilled in a cast iron skillet—delicately seasoned with salt, pepper, garlic, panko bread crumbs, lemon juice, and blessed ever so lightly with grated smoked Gouda—these may become your new appetizer of choice!

---

12 fresh oysters
¼ cup panko bread crumbs
Cracked black pepper
Kosher salt
3 garlic cloves, minced

1 small lemon
2 tablespoons unsalted butter
1 cup shredded smoked Gouda
    cheese

---

1. Carefully shuck your oysters and place them over ice until you are ready to charbroil. Heat the oven broiler.

2. Heat a cast iron skillet or grill pan over high heat. Place the oysters shell side down on the hot skillet or grill.

3. Hit each oyster with some panko, a sprinkle of pepper, salt, and a little bit of minced garlic. Squeeze some lemon juice over the oysters and ½ teaspoon of butter each. As the butter melts, grate the cheese over the oysters and let it begin to melt. Let the oysters cook for 8–10 minutes.

4. Remove the oysters from the griddle or skillet. Place them on a rimmed baking sheet and put them under the broiler so the cheese gets golden brown and bubbly. This will happen fast, so make sure not to let them burn. Serve immediately.

Nashville Hot Chicken Tacos
with Creamy Coleslaw | **SERVES 6**

ON ONE OF MY EARLIEST TRIPS TO NASHVILLE, I came across a dish that changed my life forever—Nashville hot chicken! The Music City sure knows how to balance fiery peppers and hot sauce with the right amount of sweet and savory spices to give fried chicken an unforgettable identity. In this recipe, I've created a taco filled with crunchy fried chicken bites tossed in that unique peppery sauce and topped it with creamy coleslaw to take the edge off—the spice won't hurt you, but it *will* leave a lasting impression!

Creamy Coleslaw
1 large carrot, cut into ribbons
½ head green cabbage, thinly sliced
1 cup mayonnaise
1 teaspoon granulated sugar
Kosher salt to taste
Cracked black pepper to taste

Fried Chicken
Vegetable oil, for frying
1 pound boneless skinless chicken
    breasts, cut into large chunks
Kosher salt
Cracked black pepper
2 cups all-purpose flour
12 (4-inch) flour tortillas

Spicy Sauce
8 tablespoons (1 stick) unsalted
    butter
¼ cup light brown sugar
1 tablespoon garlic powder
1 tablespoon onion powder
2 teaspoons granulated sugar
2 teaspoons cayenne pepper
1 teaspoon smoked paprika
½ teaspoon crushed red pepper
Pinch dried oregano
¾ cup your favorite hot sauce
2 tablespoons avocado oil

Southern Inspired

1. In a large bowl, combine all the creamy coleslaw ingredients and toss everything together to evenly coat. Taste and adjust seasoning as needed. Cover and refrigerate until ready to serve.

2. Pour vegetable oil into a large, heavy-bottomed pot or Dutch oven to no more than halfway up the side. Prop or clip in a deep-fry thermometer so the bulb is submerged in the oil. Heat over high heat until the thermometer registers 350 degrees F. (Alternatively, you can use a deep fryer.) Set a wire rack over a rimmed baking sheet.

3. Season the chicken with salt and pepper.

4. Pour the flour into a large bowl or a plastic bag. Toss the chicken pieces in the flour to coat thoroughly.

5. Working in batches if necessary, add the chicken to the hot oil and fry until the breading is golden brown and the chicken is cooked through, about 10 minutes. Transfer the chicken to the rack.

6. To make the spicy sauce, melt the butter in a wok or large skillet over medium-high heat. Add the remaining sauce ingredients and bring to a simmer. Toss the chicken pieces in the sauce to coat evenly.

7. Warm the flour tortillas for 1–2 minutes on each side in a dry sauté pan or griddle over medium heat.

8. To assemble the tacos, place some hot chicken in the center of each tortilla and top with coleslaw.

East Asian–Inspired Taco Bowls | SERVES 5-6

THIS RECIPE IS IDEAL FOR WHEN YOU want to up the ante on both flavor and fancy. Flavor because this dish calls upon a crisp and tangy slaw of beautiful baby bok choy, red cabbage, rice wine vinegar, sweet Thai chili sauce, honey, and sesame oil—served atop flank or skirt steak strips sautéed with fragrant ginger, garlic, onions, chili paste, and brown sugar. Fancy because the steak and slaw are served in easy-to-prepare individual baked flour tortilla bowls that you can prep and pop into the oven yourself. A truly dazzling starter!

Spicy Slaw
1 cup thinly sliced baby bok choy
1 cup thinly sliced purple cabbage
1 medium carrot, shredded
1 serrano pepper, seeded and thinly sliced
2 scallions, thinly sliced (optional)
½ cup sweet rice wine vinegar
⅓ cup avocado oil
2 tablespoons sweet Thai chili sauce
1 tablespoon honey
1 tablespoon Dijon mustard
½ teaspoon toasted sesame oil
1 tablespoon light brown sugar
Kosher salt
Cracked black pepper

Taco Bowls
10–12 (4-5 inch) flour tortillas
8 ounces flank or skirt steak, thinly sliced
2 garlic cloves, roughly chopped
1 tablespoon minced fresh ginger
2½ tablespoons light brown sugar
1½ tablespoons low-sodium soy sauce
1 tablespoon honey
1 teaspoon your favorite chili paste
Kosher salt
Cracked black pepper
2 tablespoons vegetable oil
1 yellow onion, small diced
Black sesame seeds, for garnish

1. To make the spicy slaw, in a large bowl, toss together the bok choy, cabbage, carrot, serrano, and scallions (if using).

2. In a medium bowl, whisk together the rice wine vinegar, avocado oil, Thai chili sauce, honey, Dijon mustard, sesame oil, brown sugar, salt and pepper to taste.

(continued)

3. Pour the dressing over the slaw mixture and toss to combine. The slaw can be made up to 2 days ahead; cover and refrigerate until ready to serve.

4. Preheat the oven to 350 degrees F. Spray a 12-cup nonstick muffin pan and both sides of each tortilla with cooking spray. Gently push a tortilla into each cup. (Alternatively, you can use two muffin tins, upside down, to shape the cups. Spray the bottoms of the tins and push the tortillas into the spaces between the cups to shape.) Bake the tortillas for 10–15 minutes or until lightly golden.

5. To make the filling, in a large bowl, toss the steak with the garlic, ginger, brown sugar, soy sauce, honey, chili paste, and salt and pepper to taste.

6. Heat the vegetable oil in a large skillet over medium-high heat. Add the onion and sauté until lightly golden brown, 4–5 minutes.

7. Add the seasoned steak and cook, breaking up the meat with a spoon, until browned, 4–6 minutes.

8. Divide the meat mixture between the tortilla bowls. Top with the spicy slaw and garnish with black sesame seeds.

Southern Inspired

Black Bean and Turkey Bacon Quesadillas | SERVES 5

THIS WAS ONE OF THE FIRST DISHES I ever made for my parents. I have to credit my godmother, who was also my home ec teacher, Miss Rose Thompson (that's right, I took home ec, and look at me now!). She encouraged me to try new foods and come up with a personal approach to preparing them, much as my family did. Back then I used red beans and Creole seasoning, ingredients that were second nature to me, to give the quesadilla my personal stamp. For this recipe I've used traditional black beans but called upon barbecue sauce, smoked paprika, turkey bacon, and spicy notes of chili powder to give this version a Southern twist. But if you want to share in my nostalgia, try some red beans—you can never go wrong with red beans!

12–16 slices turkey bacon, chopped
1 small red onion, diced
2 garlic cloves, minced
2 (15-ounce) cans black beans, drained and rinsed
½ cup roughly chopped fresh cilantro
2 tablespoons chili powder
2 tablespoons smoked paprika
2 tablespoons garlic powder
1 tablespoon ground cumin

½ cup your favorite barbecue sauce
Kosher salt
Cracked black pepper
10 (8-inch) flour tortillas
1½–2 cups shredded cheddar cheese
1½–2 cups shredded mozzarella cheese
Sour cream or crème fraîche, for serving
Sliced scallions, for garnish (optional)

1. In a large skillet, sauté the bacon over medium-high heat until crispy, 3–5 minutes. Add the onion and garlic and cook for a few seconds, just until fragrant. Add the beans, cilantro, chili powder, smoked paprika, garlic powder, cumin, and barbecue sauce and mix to combine. Season with salt and pepper as desired. Remove the skillet from the heat.

(continued)

2. Place a tortilla in the bottom of a nonstick skillet over medium heat. Add a layer of cheddar cheese, some of the bean and bacon filling, and then some mozzarella cheese. Place another tortilla on top. Cook for a few minutes, then carefully flip the quesadilla and cook for a few minutes on the other side, until the tortillas are golden brown and the cheese has melted. Repeat with the remaining tortillas, filling, and cheese.

3. Cut the quesadillas into wedges. Drizzle with sour cream or crème fraîche and garnish with scallions (if using).

Southern Inspired

CHAPTER 4

JUST
Hands

I TITLED THIS CHAPTER "JUST HANDS" FOR MANY REASONS. AS African Americans, we were forced to use our hands to build the foundation of this country centuries ago; throughout the years our hands have endured great pain while creating immense beauty. I come from a long line of proud family members who've used their hands for community building through farming, nursing, carpentry, fellowship, and culinary expertise.

People join hands in a show of solidarity. Loved ones show affection to one another by holding hands, and a handshake can signal a hello, a goodbye, or congratulations. But your hands can also make eating a lot of fun, especially for those dishes where a knife and fork would be inappropriate!

My family lived in Mississippi while I was growing up, but we were originally from Chicago. There's something about that city, with its rich culture and food—it gets into your pores and never leaves. When we took trips to Chicago to visit family, my dad *had* to stop off near Maxwell Street before we piled into the car to head back home. That part of town was known for its historically Eastern European roots and cuisine, and at the top of my dad's list was picking up a Polish sausage sandwich smothered in onions. Stepping into just about any restaurant, you'd be immediately captivated by the smell of those sautéed onions, the sound of sizzling sausages, the chatter of the crowds, and the sight of customers waiting for their sandwiches—seared flat-top bread, Polish sausage, sautéed onions, and mustard—simple perfection!

By the time we got back to Michigan City, Mississippi, with its cow pastures and cornfields, Chicago was a distant memory. But my dad would still ache for his beloved sausage and onions, so he did what he did best— out came that cast iron skillet! The smell of those sausages and onions cooking was hypnotic. I'd lose my mind sometimes and want to grab one straight from the pan, but my dad would always stop me and tell me to be patient and wait for the bread. But to me, the bread was almost an afterthought. Good thing that with age comes wisdom *and* patience.

When it comes to my cooking style, I can't help but share my Southern roots, making my dishes Southern inspired.

For my sausage and peppers recipe and the other five dishes in this chapter, clear your schedule, put your phones down, and get your napkins ready—all hands on deck!

Chicago-Style Southern Sausage and Peppers | SERVES 8

A CLASSIC IS A CLASSIC, AND A CHICAGO sausage and peppers sandwich is a classic. But if there's one thing I learned from my family growing up, it was to take something you love—even if it was perfection to begin with—and change it up to make it your own. Here, I've added jalapeños for an extra kick and braised the sausages in lager and Worcestershire sauce to give this sandwich a face-lift. If you can find it, braise your sausages in Louisiana's own Abita beer to make this dish truly Southern inspired.

2 pounds Italian sausage links

½ cup lager (such as Abita Amber Lager)

¼ cup water

¼ cup Worcestershire sauce

2 medium yellow onions, sliced

1 red bell pepper, julienned

2 jalapeños, julienned

3 tablespoons light brown sugar

2 tablespoons unsalted butter

8 split-top hot dog buns

1. Put the sausages in a large skillet and add the lager, water, and Worcestershire. The sausages should be half submerged. You can always add a little more lager or water if needed. Bring to a light boil over medium heat, cover the pan, and steam the sausages for about 10 minutes.

2. Add the onions, bell pepper, jalapeños, brown sugar, and butter and stir to combine. Cook, uncovered, until the onions wilt and the liquid reduces, about another 10 minutes.

3. Serve each sausage link in a split-top hot dog bun with the onion and pepper mixture on top.

Georgia Peach Hot Chicken Sandwich | SERVES 6

TWO CITIES THAT ARE NEAR AND DEAR to my heart are Nashville and Atlanta. Both places have their own charm, personality, and, of course, signature dishes. I shared with you my love for Nashville hot chicken with my Nashville Hot Chicken Tacos recipe on page 66. Here, I'm building upon greatness by complementing the chicken's fiery crunch with the sweet juiciness of peaches. Peaches aren't unique to Atlanta but known statewide in Georgia—it is, after all, the Peach State. In this recipe, I add peach syrup from canned peaches to the spicy butter glaze and top each sandwich with sautéed peaches. I hope someone is standing next to you when you take that first bite, because your knees just might buckle—it's that good!

Vegetable oil, for frying
6 (8-ounce) boneless, skin-on
   chicken breasts
Kosher salt
Ground white pepper
2 cups heavy cream
¼ cup your favorite hot sauce
2 cups all-purpose flour
2 teaspoons smoked paprika
1 teaspoon dried oregano
1 teaspoon dried thyme
1 teaspoon garlic powder
1 teaspoon cayenne pepper
Mayonnaise, for serving
6 potato buns

Bread and butter pickles, for serving
1 (15-ounce) can sliced peaches,
   syrup reserved

Spicy Butter
8 tablespoons (1 stick) unsalted
   butter
¼ cup canned peach syrup
3 tablespoons cayenne pepper
3 tablespoons light brown sugar
1 tablespoon smoked paprika
1½ teaspoons garlic powder
1 teaspoon chili powder
Kosher salt to taste
Ground white pepper to taste

---

1. Pour vegetable oil into a large, heavy-bottomed pot or Dutch oven to no more than halfway up the side. Prop or clip in a deep-fry thermometer so that the bulb is submerged in the oil. Heat over high heat until the thermometer registers 350 degrees F. (Alternatively, you can use a deep fryer.)

Southern Inspired

2. Put the chicken in a large bowl and season with salt and white pepper as desired. Add the heavy cream and hot sauce and mix to coat.

3. In another large bowl, whisk together the flour, smoked paprika, oregano, thyme, garlic powder, and cayenne.

4. Set a wire rack in a rimmed baking sheet. Remove the chicken breasts from the liquid and dip them into the flour mixture. Shake off any excess flour and gently lower the chicken into the hot oil. Working in batches, fry until the breading is golden brown and the internal temperature of the chicken reaches 165 degrees F, 12–15 minutes. Transfer the chicken to the rack.

5. Meanwhile, to make the spicy butter, melt the butter in a small saucepan over medium-high heat. Add the remaining spicy butter ingredients and bring to a boil. Let the sauce reduce for 3–5 minutes.

6. Put the fried chicken in a large bowl and gently toss with the spicy butter.

7. To assemble the sandwiches, spread mayo on each half of the buns, place pickles on the bottom, top with a chicken breast, and add a slice of canned peach. Serve right away and enjoy!

Crab Cake Texas Toast Burger | SERVES 4

WHEN I SAY TEXAS, what do you think of? I think *big*—and this recipe will leave you with four *big* and juicy burgers made with lump and claw crabmeat, dressed with a creamy peppery Cajun sauce, and served on—what else?—Texas toast. Serve these burgers with my Citrusy Lime Margarita on page 211, because no one is going home when you serve these superstars!

8 ounces crab claw meat
8 ounces lump crabmeat
½ cup panko bread crumbs
1 shallot, minced
3 tablespoons minced fresh chives
½ cup mayonnaise
2 large eggs, beaten
2 tablespoons Worcestershire sauce
1 tablespoon fresh lemon or lime juice
1 teaspoon spicy mustard
Kosher salt
Cracked black pepper
3–4 tablespoons olive oil
2–4 tablespoons unsalted butter

8 slices Texas toast bread
Butter lettuce or arugula, for assembling
Lemon wedges, for serving

Cajun Sauce

1 cup mayonnaise
2 teaspoons grated lemon or lime zest
3 dashes your favorite hot sauce
1 tablespoon prepared horseradish
1 tablespoon sweet pickle relish
2 teaspoons Cajun seasoning, homemade (page 20) or store-bought

1. In a large bowl, combine the claw and lump crabmeat, panko, shallot, chives, mayonnaise, eggs, Worcestershire, lime juice, and mustard and season with salt and pepper as desired. Mold the mixture into four even crab cakes.

2. Heat a thin layer of oil in a large skillet over medium-high heat. Sear the crab cakes until golden, 5–6 minutes per side. Transfer to a wire rack.

3. In a small bowl, combine all the Cajun sauce ingredients and stir well.

Southern Inspired

4. Melt the butter on a griddle or in a skillet over medium heat. Working in batches, add the slices of bread and toast until browned and crisp, 1–2 minutes a side, adding more butter if needed.

5. To assemble the burgers, spread the Cajun sauce on each piece of toast. Layer four slices with lettuce, then a crab cake, and more sauce on top of the crab cake. Top with the other slices of toast and serve with lemon wedges on the side.

Note: You can also serve these crab cakes without the bread and with the sauce and lemon on the side!

"The Big Juicy" Smoked Gouda Cheeseburger | SERVES 4

WELCOME TO MY TAKE ON A FAMOUS Minneapolis signature cheeseburger you might've heard of—the Jucy Lucy. "The Big Juicy" is a nod to this iconic burger, but my version gives you something to write home about! I start with garlic powder, onion powder, and smoked paprika to give the patties a flavor boost, then I call upon the goodness of smoked Gouda and provolone to take this burger to gooey new heights. But it doesn't stop there. To finish this stacked behemoth, I "turn up the Southern" by smothering it with onions sautéed in butter, Worcestershire sauce, and brown sugar. This is what you want!

Griddled Onions
2 tablespoons unsalted butter
2 sweet yellow onions, sliced
¼ cup Worcestershire sauce
1 teaspoon light brown sugar

Burgers
2 pounds 80% lean ground sirloin
2 tablespoons smoked paprika
2 teaspoons garlic powder
2 teaspoons onion powder

Kosher salt
Cracked black pepper
8 slices smoked Gouda cheese
4 slices provolone cheese
3–4 tablespoons olive oil (optional)
Bread and butter pickles, for assembling
4 brioche buns, split
1 large red onion, thinly sliced
Your favorite burger toppings and condiments

1. To make the griddled onions, melt the butter in a medium sauté pan over medium-high heat. Add the yellow onions and sauté until they are soft and translucent, about 5 minutes. Add the Worcestershire sauce and brown sugar and sauté until the onions are very soft and browned, another 5–10 minutes. (You can make the onions up to an hour ahead of time and let them sit in the pan until ready to serve.)

2. Meanwhile, in a large chilled bowl, season the meat with the smoked paprika, garlic powder, onion powder, and salt and pepper as desired. Gently mix to combine.

(continued)

3. Form the meat into eight equal patties. Create an indentation in the center of four of the patties using your fingers. Fill each indentation with 1 slice of Gouda and 1 slice of provolone. Place the remaining burger patties on top and pinch the outer edges to seal in the cheese between the patties.

4. Heat a griddle, cast iron skillet, or large nonstick skillet over high heat. (I normally sear the burgers directly on the griddle or skillet, but you can cook the burgers in olive oil if you like.) Add the burgers and cook until the underside is golden brown, about 5 minutes. The burgers may begin to swell up once the cheese starts to melt. Some of the ooey-gooey cheese may ooze out, and that is fine! Flip the burgers and top with the remaining slices of Gouda. Cook until the burgers are browned on the other side and the cheese has melted, about 5 minutes more.

5. To assemble the burgers, place pickles on the bottom bun, add the burger, and top with some red onion and a forkful of the caramelized onions. Feel free to add any other toppings and condiments you like (sliced tomato, ketchup, mustard, mayo, barbecue sauce . . .). Serve the burgers right away.

Note: I recommend serving these burgers with your favorite barbecue kettle chips on the side.

Over-the-Top Lime BBQ Shrimp Tacos | SERVES 4–6

I DIDN'T FORGET YOU, my pescatarians—this dish is for you! Zesty and light, these tacos dress pan-seared shrimp in homemade barbecue sauce before topping them with shredded cabbage, white onions, jalapeños, cilantro, and cotija cheese. If you don't have cotija cheese on hand, try substituting queso blanco, or feta for a sharp kick. Get 'em while they're hot!

Lime Barbecue Sauce
½ cup ketchup
¼ cup fresh lime juice
¼ cup light brown sugar
1 tablespoon liquid smoke
1 tablespoon chili powder

Shrimp Tacos
1 pound large shrimp, peeled and
    deveined

3 tablespoons olive oil
8–10 (4-inch) flour tortillas
1 cup shredded purple cabbage
¼ cup small-diced white onion
1–2 jalapeños, julienned
⅓ cup crumbled cotija cheese
Fresh cilantro leaves, for garnish
    (optional)
Lime wedges, for serving

1. Mix all the lime barbecue sauce ingredients in a medium bowl.

2. Add the shrimp to the sauce and toss to coat.

3. Heat the oil in a large sauté pan over medium-high heat. Add the shrimp and sear on both sides until they're opaque and pink, 3–4 minutes. Remove from the heat.

4. Heat the mini tortillas on both sides on a griddle over medium-high heat until warm and pliable, 1–2 minutes.

5. To assemble the tacos, place 2–3 shrimp on each tortilla. Top with shredded cabbage, white onion, jalapeño, cotija cheese, and cilantro. Serve with lime wedges on the side.

Southern Inspired

Jernard's Showstopper Chicago-Style Cheesesteak | SERVES 4-6

I DON'T THROW THE WORD *showstopper* around carelessly; I reserve it for exceptional circumstances and dishes. In this case, I'm proud to share my recipe for this extraordinary sandwich. It starts with thinly sliced rib eye steak and builds with a crescendo of sautéed onions and peppers—bathed in a silky provolone and smoked cheddar cheese sauce—and topped off with a nod to my Chicago roots, pickled giardiniera. OK, I'll say it again: it's a showstopper!

1–2 tablespoons avocado oil
½ yellow bell pepper, julienned
½ green bell pepper, julienned
1 yellow onion, sliced
Kosher salt
Cracked black pepper
2 pounds boneless rib eye steak, thinly sliced against the grain
3 tablespoons Worcestershire sauce

6 tablespoons unsalted butter
¼ cup all-purpose flour
2 cups heavy cream
1 cup shredded provolone cheese
1 cup shredded smoked cheddar cheese
1 (18-inch) sub roll
2 cups giardiniera, drained

---

1. Heat the avocado oil in a large sauté pan over medium-high heat. Add the peppers and onion and sauté until they soften and begin to get very brown, about 5 minutes. Season with salt and black pepper as desired.

2. Season the steak with salt and pepper and add to the peppers and onion. Cook until the steak is tender, 5–10 minutes. Stir in the Worcestershire sauce and remove the pan from the heat.

3. In a medium saucepan, melt the butter over medium-high heat. Add the flour and cook, whisking constantly, for about 4 minutes to form a roux. Whisk in the heavy cream, making sure there are no lumps. Add the cheese and stir until melted. Remove from the heat.

4. Slice the sub roll in half but not all the way through. Fill with the steak, peppers, and onion, top with the giardiniera, and pour the cheese sauce evenly over the top.

CHAPTER 5

"LET IT GO"
One-Pot MEALS

*T*HERE IS BEAUTY TO A SEASONED, WELL-LOVED CAST IRON pot. Not beauty in the traditional sense of the word, but beauty in the rich history and meaning to families who've been lucky enough to pass skillets and Dutch ovens down from one generation to the next. The tradition of one-pot cooking traveled with enslaved Africans to the plantations of the South, where stewed dishes like gumbo and jambalaya were created—resulting in the birth of Cajun and Creole cuisines.

The way I see it, each meal you make in a cast iron pot adds another chapter to its story, informing but never outshining the next dish. It holds the joy and connection of past meals—and that's a beautiful thing!

When I was growing up, a cast iron pot was the only kind of pot my family cooked with. It didn't matter if it was crab cakes, lamb chops, mac and cheese, or cobbler, that skillet or Dutch oven was front and center, knowing what needed to be done, waiting patiently for the games to begin. Everybody understood what it meant when they saw that cast iron pot and smelled those onions sautéing—Lil Momma or Matt was fixing to get busy!

We ate gumbo all year round, but there was something about the colder months that made it taste that much better. My dad became disabled later in life and was unable to work, but he could still cook—and boy, did he cook! All week he'd put aside leftovers from roast chicken or sausage dinners and come Friday, I'd get home from school, see that cast iron Dutch oven, smell those onions frying, and I *knew* it was time for gumbo! I'd work as his sous chef, learning his secrets along the way as he added the past week's treasures to the pot with shrimp, vegetables, and his special blend of fresh herbs and spices—and sometimes, he'd even let me help prepare the roux.

Anybody who cooks gumbo knows that roux is the foundation of this dish, and if you don't get your roux right, it's just wrong. People have debated right and wrong roux for hundreds of years. See, roux can run from white all the way to cocoa brown. Cajun or Creole. Some people say the darker the roux . . . All I know is, Matt's roux was always right!

My dad left some pretty big shoes to fill, but it has been my honor to build upon his legacy as I share my recipe for Gumbo with My Father and eight other one-pot wonders that will help you slow down, gather around the table, and connect.

Gumbo with My Father | SERVES 6-8

MY LATE FATHER, MATT, was many things to many people. But to me, he was my role model and confidant. Ask anyone who knew him—he was always good for an outrageous story, a meaningful lesson, or a side-splitting laugh. This recipe reminds me of him each time I make it. And in just the same way my dad was a real character, the addition of smoked oysters and turkey legs brings a unique quality to this favorite that is unmistakable. I hope this dish brings much joy and laughter to your table as you enjoy it with friends and family—Matt would be honored.

Southern Inspired

1 cup vegetable oil

6 boneless, skinless chicken breasts, cut into strips

Kosher salt

Cracked black pepper

6 chicken andouille sausage links, cut into ½-inch pieces

¼ cup roughly chopped garlic

6 tablespoons unsalted butter

1 cup all-purpose flour

1 medium yellow onion, small diced

1 yellow bell pepper, small diced

1 cup small-diced celery

1 quart chicken broth

1 (12-ounce) bottle lager beer (such as Abita Amber Lager)

2 tablespoons gumbo filé

4 ounces smoked oysters, roughly chopped

2 medium smoked turkey legs, skin and bones discarded, meat roughly chopped

1½ pounds medium shrimp, peeled and deveined

3–4 cups cooked white rice, for serving

Chopped fresh scallions or parsley, for garnish

1. Heat the oil in a large, heavy-bottomed pot or Dutch oven over medium-high heat. Add the chicken and season with salt and pepper as desired. Cook, turning once halfway through cooking, until the chicken is golden brown on both sides, 5–6 minutes. Transfer the chicken to a plate.

2. Add the sausage to the pot and cook for 3–4 minutes to render the fat. Transfer the sausage to another plate.

3. Add the garlic to the pot and sauté until the garlic is aromatic, about 1 minute. Add the butter and let it melt. Add the flour and cook, stirring continuously, until a dark chocolate–colored roux forms, 10–15 minutes.

4. Add the onion, bell pepper, and celery to the roux and stir to combine. Add the chicken broth, beer, and gumbo filé and whisk or stir to avoid lumps. Bring to a low simmer.

5. Add the oysters, smoked turkey, and chicken and stir while the mixture comes back up to a simmer. Reduce the heat to medium, cover the pot, and cook for 15–20 minutes until the vegetables have softened and the gumbo has thickened.

6. Once the gumbo is just about ready, add the shrimp and cook until they are tender and cooked through, about 5 minutes.

7. Serve the gumbo with white rice and garnish with scallions and/or parsley.

Oxtails and Bow Ties | SERVES 4–6

OXTAILS NEED TIME TO SLOW COOK into a melt-in-your-mouth, fla-vorsome stew. As a child I remember waiting very impatiently for my mom's oxtails to finish simmering in her favorite cast iron Dutch oven. I couldn't understand why they took so long, but after my first bite it didn't matter, because the reward for waiting was found in every mouth-ful. Here, I've added butter beans and bow tie pasta to complement this favorite comfort food.

4 pounds meaty oxtails
Kosher salt
Cracked black pepper
½ cup all-purpose flour
3 tablespoons avocado or vegetable oil
2 carrots (preferably one orange and one white), sliced ½ inch thick
1 medium yellow onion, medium diced
4 garlic cloves, rough chopped
1 cup dry red wine
½ cup Tennessee whiskey

3 cups beef stock
¼ cup Worcestershire sauce
4 tablespoons (½ stick) unsalted butter
¼ cup loosely packed light brown sugar
1 teaspoon ground allspice
1 teaspoon grated fresh ginger
1 cup heavy cream
1 (15-ounce) can butter beans, drained and rinsed
1 pound bow tie pasta, cooked
Fresh rosemary, for garnish

1. In a large bowl, season the oxtails with salt and pepper. Sprinkle the flour over the oxtails and toss to coat.

2. Put the oxtails in a large Dutch oven and cook until golden brown, 5–6 minutes on each side. Transfer the oxtails to a plate.

3. Heat the oil in the Dutch oven over medium-high heat. Add the carrots, onion, and garlic and cook for 3–4 minutes so the carrots begin to soften.

Southern Inspired

4. Pour in the red wine and whiskey and deglaze for about 2 minutes.

5. Add the beef stock, Worcestershire, butter, brown sugar, allspice, and ginger and stir to combine. Return the oxtails to the pot, cover, and bring to a simmer. Lower the heat to medium-low and cook until the oxtails are tender and falling off the bone, 2½–3 hours.

6. Add the heavy cream, butter beans, and pasta and cook just until heated through. Garnish with fresh rosemary.

Three-Alarm Chili
with Avocado Ranch | **SERVES 4-6**

THIS DISH HAS A SECRET. Your guests will think you're serving them the most satisfying, *slow-cooked*, scrumptious spicy chili—balanced perfectly with a dollop of healthy and cooling avocado ranch. What they won't know is that you whipped up this undeniably tasty crowd-pleaser in less than an hour with ingredients easily found in your pantry. This is the perfect "anytime is chili time" recipe!

---

2 tablespoons avocado oil
1 large yellow onion, small diced
1 red bell pepper, small diced
2 medium celery stalks, small diced
1 serrano pepper, finely chopped
2 tablespoons minced garlic
Kosher salt
Cracked black pepper
2 pounds 80% lean ground beef
3 tablespoons chili powder
1 tablespoon ground cumin
1 tablespoon dried oregano

2 teaspoons onion powder
1 teaspoon garlic powder
½ teaspoon cayenne pepper
2 bay leaves
3 cups diced fresh tomatoes
1 (15-ounce) can black beans with liquid
1 (15-ounce) can red kidney beans with liquid
2 cups chicken broth
Shredded Manchego cheese, for serving (optional)

---

1. Heat the oil in a large skillet or sauté pan over medium-high heat. Add the onion, bell pepper, celery, serrano pepper, and garlic and sauté until the onion is translucent, 3–4 minutes. Season with salt and pepper as desired.

2. Add the meat, breaking it up with the back of your spoon and stirring it into the vegetables. Add the chili powder, cumin, oregano, onion powder, garlic powder, cayenne, and bay leaves. Season again with salt and pepper as desired. Stir everything to combine.

3. Add the tomatoes, black beans with their liquid, kidney beans with their liquid, and chicken broth. Bring the chili to a simmer and cook for 15–20 minutes.

4. Remove the bay leaves and serve topped with Manchego cheese and a dollop of avocado ranch (recipe follows).

Southern Inspired

Avocado Ranch

½ cup sour cream

¼ cup pureed or mashed avocado

¼ cup mayonnaise

1 tablespoon buttermilk

1 tablespoon dried dill

2 teaspoons onion powder

2 teaspoons garlic powder

2 teaspoons sugar

1 teaspoon dried parsley

Salt

1. In a small bowl, stir together the sour cream, avocado, mayonnaise, and buttermilk.

2. Add the dill, onion powder, garlic powder, sugar, and parsley. Season with salt to taste.

3. Cover and refrigerate until ready to serve.

NOLA-Style BBQ Shrimp | SERVES 4-6

THIS IS AN ENTRÉE THAT I'LL ORDER whenever I see it on a menu. This shrimp dish ticks all the boxes—flavor, texture, aroma, and beauty. It brings the heat "NOLA style," with hot sauce, Cajun seasoning, crushed red pepper, and cayenne pepper—yet remains balanced with notes of brown sugar, garlic, and herbs. But you don't need to travel to Louisiana to enjoy this dish—reach for this recipe to bring a little of that New Orleans spirit into your own kitchen. Baked in a 400-degree oven under a canopy of sliced lemons, this dish is best served with garlic bread and your favorite chilled white wine.

4 tablespoons (½ stick) unsalted butter

¼ cup minced garlic

½ cup Worcestershire sauce

¼ cup your favorite hot sauce

1 tablespoon light brown sugar

1 teaspoon dried thyme

1 tablespoon paprika

1 tablespoon Cajun seasoning, homemade (page 20) or store-bought

2 teaspoons onion powder

1 teaspoon crushed red pepper

½ teaspoon cayenne pepper

2 bay leaves

2 pounds jumbo shrimp, deveined but unpeeled

1 large lemon, sliced

Garlic bread, for serving

1. Preheat the oven to 400 degrees F.

2. Melt the butter in a large cast iron skillet over medium-high heat. Add the garlic and saute for 1 minute. Stir in the Worcestershire, hot sauce, brown sugar, thyme, and spices. Allow the seasonings and sugar to cook down and simmer for about 5 minutes.

3. Add the shrimp to the pan, making sure to coat them evenly in the sauce. Lay the lemon slices over the shrimp. Cover the pan with aluminum foil and bake for 10 minutes or until the shrimp are cooked through.

4. Remove the bay leaves and serve with your favorite garlic bread.

Southern-Inspired Spanish Chicken with Rice | SERVES 4-6

HERE I TAKE ARROZ CON POLLO and add some cocina sureña (Southern cooking) with Louisiana hot sauce, Cajun seasoning, and beautiful Carolina Gold rice to make this chicken and rice dish a Southern-inspired family favorite. Complete your meal by serving it with my Zesty Coleslaw for balanced bites of savory, sweet, and sharp.

Southern-Inspired Spice Blend
- 2¼ teaspoons onion powder
- 2¼ teaspoons garlic powder
- 2 teaspoons Cajun seasoning, homemade (page 20) or store-bought
- 1½ teaspoons chili powder
- 1½ teaspoons smoked paprika
- ¾ teaspoon ground cumin
- ¾ teaspoon ground coriander
- ½ teaspoon cayenne pepper
- ½ teaspoon dried thyme

Chicken and Rice
- 1 (3½–4-pound) chicken, cut into 8 serving pieces
- Kosher salt
- Cracked black pepper
- 2 tablespoons agave syrup, divided
- 2–3 tablespoons olive oil
- 1 cup uncooked parboiled Carolina Gold rice
- 2 lemons
- 2 cups low-sodium chicken broth
- 2 tablespoons hot sauce
- Small bunch cilantro, minced

1. In a small bowl, combine the ingredients for the spice blend.

2. In a large bowl, season the chicken pieces with salt and pepper as desired, 1 tablespoon of the spice blend, and 1 tablespoon of the agave.

3. Heat the olive oil in a large nonstick skillet over medium-high to high heat. Add the chicken pieces, skin-side down. Cover the pan and sear the chicken for about 5 minutes on each side. Transfer the chicken to a plate (it won't be cooked through at this point).

4. In the same pan, toast the parboiled rice in the chicken juices, stirring, for 1–2 minutes. Add the juice of 1 lemon, chicken broth, hot sauce, another 1 tablespoon of the spice blend, remaining 1 tablespoon agave, and salt and pepper as desired, and stir to combine.

Southern Inspired

5. Return the chicken to the pan. Cover and cook for 15 minutes over low heat. Uncover, raise the heat to medium, and cook until the rice has absorbed the liquid and the chicken is cooked, 10–15 minutes.

6. Cut the remaining lemon into wedges for serving. Serve the chicken with fresh lemon wedges and garnish with cilantro.

Note: The Southern-Inspired Spice Blend recipe makes twice as much as you'll need for this dish. Reserve the remainder for the next time you make this recipe! Store it in an airtight container until you're ready to use it.

Creamy Tomato Basil Soup | SERVES 4

LET ME SEE A SHOW OF HANDS for how many of you have had home-made tomato soup made from fresh tomatoes. A lot of people haven't because it's hard to shake the image of that red-and-white can from childhood and believe there can be anything better than that. But if you love tomato soup as much as I love tomato soup, then please try your hand at this super easy, 30-minutes-from-start-to-finish, bright and tasty classic. Pair it with your favorite grilled cheese sandwich for a walk down memory lane.

---

3 tablespoons unsalted butter

2 tablespoons olive oil or grapeseed oil

2 garlic cloves, coarsely minced

¾ cup (loosely packed) coarsely chopped basil leaves, divided

2–3 teaspoons light brown sugar

6 medium tomatoes, pureed

1 cup vegetable broth

3 tablespoons onion powder

2 tablespoons garlic powder

Kosher salt

Cracked black pepper

1–1½ cups heavy cream

1 medium tomato, diced, for garnish

Sour cream, for serving (optional)

---

1. Melt together the butter and oil in a large saucepan or Dutch oven over medium heat. Add the garlic, half of the basil, and brown sugar and sauté, stirring, for 2–3 minutes.

2. Whisk in the tomato puree, vegetable broth, onion powder, and garlic powder. Season with salt and pepper to taste.

3. Add the heavy cream, stir to combine, and cover the pan. Bring the soup to a simmer and cook for 15 minutes.

4. Serve the soup topped with the remaining basil, diced tomatoes, and a dollop of sour cream, if you like.

Southern Inspired

Curry Chicken Stew with Potatoes and Veggies | SERVES 4-6

EVEN THOUGH CURRY DISHES CAN BE FOUND in many cultures, this dish pays tribute to my Caribbean brothers and sisters. Instead of using premade curry powder, I've created my own blend with ground turmeric, coriander, allspice, and cumin—and for those willing to take the plunge, I've added a habanero pepper to keep this dish island-ready!

2 tablespoons olive oil
¼ cup small-diced onion
3 tablespoons minced garlic
1 habanero pepper, halved and
    seeded (optional)
4 boneless, skinless chicken breasts
Kosher salt
Cracked black pepper
2 cups medium-diced red potatoes
1 cup medium-diced carrots
4 cups chicken broth

1 head broccoli, cut into florets
1 teaspoon ground turmeric
1 teaspoon ground coriander
1 teaspoon ground allspice
1 teaspoon ground cumin
1 cup canned coconut milk
2 cups cooked white rice, for
    serving
Chopped fresh flat-leaf parsley, for
    garnish

1. Heat the olive oil in a large Dutch oven over medium-high heat. Sauté the onion and garlic until aromatic and golden, 2–3 minutes. Add the habanero (if using).

2. Season the chicken breasts with salt and pepper on one side. Add the chicken to the pot, seasoned-side down, then season the other side with salt and pepper. Sear the chicken for 3–4 minutes on each side to create a delicious crust. Add the potatoes and carrots (parboiled if desired) as the chicken cooks, allowing them to soak up the flavor.

3. Add the chicken broth, cover, and bring the mixture to a boil.

4. Add the broccoli florets and push them down into the boiling chicken broth. Lower to a simmer.

Southern Inspired

5. In a small bowl, mix the spices into the coconut milk so they are well blended before adding to the stew. Pour into the chicken broth and stir. Put the lid back on the pot and cook for another 10–15 minutes.

6. Remove the habanero (if used). Serve the curry over white rice and garnish with parsley.

Spicy Sizzling Skirt Steak | SERVES 4–6

HERE'S AN EASY EAST ASIAN–INSPIRED steak dish that takes very little time to prepare but leaves a lasting impression. Packed with flavor from garlic, chili paste, brown sugar, and soy sauce, and made healthier with crisp snow peas and julienned orange bell pepper, this bright and tasty rainbow dish will delight your taste buds *and* your guests'.

---

2 tablespoons grapeseed oil
1 yellow onion, thinly sliced
1 orange bell pepper, julienned
2 cups snow peas
8 garlic cloves, minced
Kosher salt
Cracked black pepper

1 pound skirt steak, thinly sliced
   against the grain
½ cup low-sodium soy sauce
2 tablespoons chili paste
2 tablespoons light brown sugar
Toasted sesame seeds, for garnish
3 cups cooked white rice, for serving

---

1. Heat the oil in a large cast iron skillet over medium-high heat. Sauté the onion, bell pepper, snow peas, and garlic until the onion is translucent and the pepper and peas begin to soften, about 5 minutes. Season with salt and pepper as desired.

2. Season the steak with salt and pepper. Add the steak to the pan and mix into the vegetables. Cook until the meat is browned, 3–5 minutes.

3. Add the soy sauce, chili paste, and brown sugar. Cook until the sauce thickens and coats the meat and vegetables, another few minutes.

4. Garnish with toasted sesame seeds and serve over white rice.

One-Pot Fettuccine and Sausage | SERVES 4–6

THIS RECIPE IS ONE OF MY FAMILY'S GO-TOS when we want plenty of flavor but have very little time. In less than 30 minutes you can prepare this easy yet satisfying pasta dish that can feed your whole family—in fact, why not double it and invite the neighbors? Pasta party time!

2 tablespoons unsalted butter	1 teaspoon cornstarch
1 tablespoon olive oil	Kosher salt
8 garlic cloves, roughly chopped	5 cups low-sodium chicken broth
1 pound Italian sausage links	1 cup tricolored grape tomatoes,
2 teaspoons garlic powder	halved
2 teaspoons onion powder	1 pound fettuccine
2 sprigs fresh thyme	Grated Parmesan cheese, for
2 sprigs fresh rosemary	serving

1. Melt the butter and olive oil together in a large, deep skillet over medium-high heat. Add the garlic and sausage, breaking up the sausage links into big chunks with your wooden spoon. Brown for 2–3 minutes. Add the garlic powder, onion powder, thyme, rosemary, cornstarch, and a little bit of salt (don't overseason—remember the sausage and broth also add salt to this dish). Stir everything together, making sure the cornstarch doesn't clump and the seasonings coat the sausage. As they brown, continue to break the sausage into smaller pieces with your spoon.

2. Pour in the chicken broth. As it comes up to a simmer, add the tomatoes.

3. When the stock is bubbling, add the fettuccine to the pan, making sure it's submerged in the liquid. Simmer until the pasta is al dente (usually about 12 minutes—follow the directions on the package) and the liquid has thickened, creating a delicious sauce.

4. Serve the pasta topped with grated Parmesan.

CHAPTER 6

JERNARD'S BANGIN'
Backyard Barbecue

*T*HE ROOTS OF BARBECUE CAN BE TRACED BACK TO THE TAINO (Indigenous peoples of the Caribbean), Native Americans, and enslaved Africans. Each group built upon techniques and spice blends of the others to create barbecue as we know it today in America. Almost ceremonial in its preparation and sanctified for its regional recipes, barbecue is entrenched as a staple of Southern culture and cuisine. Nothing brings people together like a barbecue can!

When I was growing up in Mississippi, as soon as the temperature was close enough to 69 degrees my dad would say, "Your great-grandaddy's gettin' ready to pull meat out the smokehouse—you know what that means!" It meant barbecue season had arrived, even though to me, 69 degrees was *barely* spring. My great-grandfather, Peter Young—not Peter Old, but Peter Young—got things rolling when he started taking down steaks, pork chops, legs, and loins that had been aging in his smokehouse, replacing them with fresh cuts, and divvying up the meat among friends and family for cookouts. Have you ever seen a pretty pork chop? Those were some pretty chops. I'm talking thick, juicy two-inchers, aged to smoky perfection and ready for the grill!

My great-grandparents had a peach tree that supplied us with enough fruit to eat all year round, whether fresh or home-canned. Once barbecue season kicked in, my great-grandfather and dad would grill peaches and process them into a smoky glaze that they would then drizzle over the chops when they came off the fire. Those chops, the peach glaze, and the smoke from the hickory wood that I cut myself from stumps out back left such an impression on me that I made a version of this for the "Dish of My Life" segment when I finished as runner-up on *Food Network Star*, Season 12.

But it wasn't just the dish itself that was so meaningful to me—although it really is *that* good. It was the memories of eating those chops with friends and family around the fire, feeling that warmth, that love, that community that food brings about. It was also the time when I would "ear hustle" around my aunts, uncles, and older cousins—listening to grown folks talk, being welcomed in. We were connected.

Get ready to spread some joy and make some memories as you prepare these Peach and Chipotle Glazed Pork Chops, along with five other grill favorites and three sides at your next bangin' barbecue!

Peach and Chipotle Glazed Pork Chops | SERVES 4

THIS RECIPE TAKES ME STRAIGHT BACK to my childhood. Memories of friends and family spending time together around the fire, day turning into night and nobody wanting to go home, come flooding back when I start to smell these chops sizzling on the grill with their hints of sweet peaches and smoky chipotle peppers. Don't be surprised if your guests want you to share this recipe with them. I wouldn't mind—keep spreading the love!

¼ cup canned chipotles in adobo sauce, finely chopped
1 tablespoon minced shallot
1 tablespoon minced garlic
2 tablespoons agave or honey
2 tablespoons peach puree or peach nectar

4 (1–2-inch-thick) bone-in pork chops
Kosher salt
Cracked black pepper
2 peaches, halved and pitted
Chopped fresh flat-leaf parsley, for garnish (optional)

---

1. Mix the chipotles, shallot, garlic, agave, and peach juice together in a large bowl or resealable plastic bag.

2. Season the pork chops with salt and pepper as desired. Coat the pork chops in the peach-chipotle mixture. Cover the bowl or seal the bag and refrigerate for 15–20 minutes to allow the marinade to work its way into the meat.

3. Preheat the grill to 350 degrees F. (If you do not have a grill, you can use a cast iron griddle on the stove over medium-high to high heat.)

4. Place the pork chops on the grill. Grill until the internal temperature reaches 145 degrees F (for medium to medium-well-done), about 20 minutes, flipping every 5 minutes so they do not burn. Grill the peach halves, cut-side down, just until char marks form.

5. Serve the pork chops garnished with the grilled peaches and fresh parsley, if desired.

Southern Inspired

Jerk Beef Ribs | SERVES 6–8

I'M SO THANKFUL TO MY PARENTS for introducing different kinds of foods to me and my siblings when we were growing up. We lived in the South, but our table represented a global community. My dad, Matt, was always experimenting with different spice blends and marinades to help broaden our palates, and luckily he passed down his gift of culinary creativity to me. This dish will have you dreaming of beachside rum punches as you enjoy a spicy Jamaican favorite, but don't be intimidated by the heat—it won't hurt you, but it'll get the point across!

¼ cup light brown sugar
1 tablespoon onion powder
1 tablespoon garlic powder
1 tablespoon smoked paprika
1 tablespoon ground allspice
1 tablespoon ground cinnamon
1 tablespoon cayenne pepper
1½ teaspoons dried thyme
1½ teaspoons crushed red pepper

1½ teaspoons salt
1½ teaspoons dried parsley
1½ teaspoons ground ginger
1½ teaspoons dried mustard
¾ teaspoon ground white pepper
¾ teaspoon cracked black pepper
¼ cup olive oil
6 pounds short ribs

---

1. In a medium bowl, combine all the ingredients except the ribs to form a paste.

2. Rub the ribs with the paste on both sides. Place the ribs on a large rimmed baking sheet or platter. Cover with aluminum foil or plastic wrap and marinate in the refrigerator for up to 24 hours.

3. When you're ready to cook, preheat the grill to 350 degrees F. Grill the ribs for 20 minutes, flipping them a few times during cooking so that char marks form on the outside.

4. Lower the temperature of the grill to 325 degrees F and continue to cook until the internal temperature of the ribs registers 145–150 degrees F and the meat is ready to fall off the bone, about 35–40 minutes more.

Broccoli and Cabbage Slaw | SERVES 4-6

I THINK ONE OF THE SECRETS to a healthy and happy life is balance. Balance can also elevate a dish or a meal from ordinary to extraordinary. This chapter is dedicated to all things beautifully barbecued, and my Broccoli and Cabbage Slaw is not only balanced perfectly within itself—with crunchiness from broccoli and cabbage, creaminess from mayonnaise, sweetness from a bit of sugar and sweet pickle relish, and tang from Dijon mustard—but it pairs nicely with all the recipes in this chapter by adding a light touch to balance the richness of the barbecued mains.

3 cups broccoli slaw
3 cups shredded cabbage or coleslaw mix
⅓ cup sugar
1 cup mayonnaise
½ cup sweet pickle relish
¼ cup Dijon mustard
2 tablespoons celery salt
Kosher salt to taste
Ground white pepper to taste

1. In a large bowl, combine all the ingredients until everything is well incorporated.

2. Cover and chill in the fridge for about 1 hour or until ready to serve.

Southern Inspired

Lemon Pepper Chicken Skewers | SERVES 4

SERVE THIS MILD YET FLAVORFUL DISH alongside some of my spicier mains from this chapter to help balance the *bang* in your bangin' backyard barbecue. Paired with my Southern-Style Potato Salad, this dish will keep it smooth and mellow.

---

1 pound boneless, skinless chicken thighs, cut lengthwise into thick strips

2 tablespoons lemon pepper

1 tablespoon all-purpose seasoning

3 tablespoons honey

1 lemon, sliced, for garnish (optional)

---

1. Preheat the grill or oven to 350 degrees F. If using wooden skewers, soak them in water for 30 minutes.

2. Put the chicken strips in a large bowl and season with the lemon pepper, all-purpose seasoning, and honey. Turn to coat thoroughly.

3. Thread the chicken onto skewers. You may be able to fit 2–3 strips per skewer.

4. If grilling, grill the skewers until cooked through, about 15 minutes. If baking, line a rimmed baking sheet with aluminum foil, set a rack on it, and grease the rack. Place the skewers on the rack and bake for about 25 minutes or until the internal temperature of the chicken reaches 165 degrees F.

5. Serve the skewers with lemon slices, if desired.

Cranberry-Whiskey Glazed Pork Ribs | SERVES 4–6

IF YOU'RE LOOKING TO ADD DEPTH and layers of flavor to your barbecued ribs, this recipe is for you. The whiskey helps punch up the flavors of the cranberry chipotle glaze, giving you a sweet, sour, spicy, and smoky mouthful in every bite. Pair these ribs with my Southern-Style Potato Salad to complete your barbecue lineup.

---

2 racks Saint Louis–style ribs, baby back ribs, or spare ribs
Kosher salt
Cracked black pepper
2 cups cranberry juice
1 cup Tennessee whiskey (such as Uncle Nearest Premium Whiskey)
1½ cups packed light brown sugar

¼ cup honey
¼ cup canned chipotles in adobo sauce, finely chopped
¼ cup fresh lemon juice
2 tablespoons smoked paprika
1 tablespoon minced garlic
1½ teaspoons dry mustard
Sliced scallions, for garnish (optional)

---

1. Preheat the oven to 325 degrees F.

2. Season the ribs with salt and pepper as desired. Lay them on a rimmed baking sheet, cover with aluminum foil, and bake for 2-3 hours depending on the ribs or until the ribs are fork-tender and nearly falling off the bone.

3. In the meantime, combine the remaining ingredients in a medium saucepan. Bring to a simmer over medium-high heat and cook until it reaches a syrupy consistency, 10–15 minutes. Set aside.

4. Preheat the grill to high. Grill the ribs until char marks form, 3–5 minutes per side.

5. Remove the ribs from the grill, pour the sauce over the top, and serve garnished with scallions if you like.

Chimichurri Flank Steak | SERVES 4

CHIMICHURRI WASN'T A STEAK SAUCE that I came across very often when I was growing up in Mississippi. In fact, it was my mom, Gwen, who first introduced me to this zesty Argentinian favorite. She harvested parsley and fresh herbs from her window-box garden and whipped together this beautiful, pungent sauce with local honey, garlic, and pantry items to complement our steak dinners. It was so good it made me want to tango!

½ cup chopped fresh flat-leaf parsley

½ cup chopped fresh curly parsley

½ cup chopped fresh cilantro

2 tablespoons minced scallion

2 teaspoons minced garlic

1 tablespoon minced fresh oregano leaves

1 teaspoon crushed red pepper

¼ cup rice wine vinegar

1½ tablespoons honey

2 tablespoons crushed pine nuts

½–¾ cup olive oil

Kosher salt

Cracked black pepper

2 pounds flank steak

1. In a medium bowl, combine the flat-leaf and curly parsleys, cilantro, scallion, garlic, oregano, red pepper, rice wine vinegar, honey, and pine nuts. Mix thoroughly to combine. Slowly stream in the oil, using a fork or whisk to mix it into the other ingredients all the while; adjust the amount of oil depending on whether you like your sauce tight or loose. Season with salt and pepper as desired. Set aside.

2. Preheat the grill to 350 degrees F. Season the flank steak on both sides with salt and pepper as desired. Grill the steak for 4–6 minutes per side or until the desired internal temperature is reached: 135 degrees F for medium-rare or 145 degrees F for medium.

3. Remove the flank steak and allow it to rest on a cutting board for about 10 minutes, then slice against the grain.

4. If you like, transfer the sliced steak to a serving platter. Spoon the chimichurri sauce over the top, or serve it in a bowl alongside the steak and let your guests add sauce to their liking.

Southern-Style Potato Salad | SERVES 8–10

A BARBECUE WOULDN'T BE A BARBECUE without potato salad. A Southern barbecue wouldn't be a barbecue without a Southern-style potato salad. You see, it needs the taste *and* the color to be Southern. The taste comes from thin-skinned, waxy Yukon Gold potatoes, mayonnaise, apple cider vinegar, sweet pickle relish, diced celery, Vidalia onions, sugar, and spices. The color comes from yellow mustard, smoked paprika, and boiled eggs. All combined, this makes one of the smoothest, creamiest, and tangiest potato salads around. Trust me when I tell you the potato salad is just as important as the main dish at any bangin' barbecue!

---

3 pounds Yukon Gold potatoes, peeled and cut into large chunks
Kosher salt
6 hard-cooked eggs, peeled and diced

Dressing
1¾–2 cups mayo
¾ cup sweet pickle relish
½ cup sugar

¼ cup yellow mustard
2 tablespoons apple cider vinegar
½ cup small-diced Vidalia onion
2 large celery stalks, small diced
1 small bunch fresh dill, chopped, plus more for garnish
2 teaspoons smoked paprika
½ teaspoon onion powder
Kosher salt to taste
Cracked black pepper to taste

---

1. Put the potatoes in a large pot. Add enough water to cover by about 1 inch and season with salt. Bring to a boil over high heat, then reduce the heat to medium and simmer until the potatoes are tender, about 15 minutes (be sure not to overcook them or they may get mushy). Drain and set aside in a large bowl to cool.

2. Mix all the dressing ingredients in a medium bowl.

3. Pour the dressing over the cooled potatoes and gently fold to combine everything. Transfer the potato salad to a serving platter or bowl. Scatter the eggs on top and sprinkle with more dill. Serve right away or cover and chill until ready to enjoy.

Southern Inspired

Lime Margarita Can Chicken | SERVES 4

NO NEED TO KEEP THIS DISH for Cinco de Mayo—serve this party favorite whenever you're ready to bring the fiesta to your table. The key to its crispy, golden-brown skin lies in marinating the chicken in lime margarita mix, brown sugar, spices, and olive oil before placing it over a beer can and allowing it to sit upright as it grills. Why not go all the way and serve it with my Citrusy Lime Margarita for a celebration of your very own?

2 tablespoons light brown sugar	1 tablespoon dried parsley
2 tablespoons garlic powder	¼ cup fresh lime juice
2 tablespoons onion powder	¼ cup olive oil
1 tablespoon kosher salt	1 (3–4-pound) whole chicken
1 tablespoon cracked black pepper	1 (12-ounce) can lime margarita (such
1 tablespoon smoked paprika	as Bud Light Lime-A-Rita)

1. Preheat the grill to 350 degrees F.

2. In a large bowl or container big enough to fit the chicken, mix the brown sugar, all the spices, lime juice, and olive oil together to create a paste. Rub the paste all over the chicken.

3. Open the margarita and place the can in a special beer can chicken holder or rack. Place the chicken over the beer can and sit it upright on the grill. Close the lid and grill for 1½–2 hours or until the skin is brown and crispy and the internal temperature of the chicken reaches 165 degrees F.

4. Carefully remove the chicken from the grill. Remove the chicken from the can and allow to rest for about 15 minutes before carving.

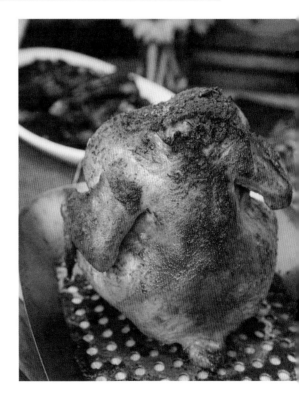

Meaty Maple Baked Beans | SERVES 6-8

I LIKE THROWING CURVE BALLS into my cooking, giving you something that you're not expecting. Case in point, my Meaty Maple Baked Beans. For starters, I use canned kidney beans instead of traditional navy beans. Then I simmer the beans with sautéed ground beef, red bell pepper, yellow bell pepper, scallions, garlic, brown sugar, maple syrup, and barbecue sauce. It's a meal within a meal that can be served as a supporting cast member or the star of your show—you decide!

1 tablespoon olive oil
1 pound 80% lean ground beef
1 red bell pepper, diced
1 yellow bell pepper, diced
2 scallions, sliced
1 tablespoon minced garlic

2 (15-ounce) cans kidney beans, drained and rinsed
½ cup maple syrup
½ cup your favorite barbecue sauce (I recommend Chef Jernard's Mesquite Golden BBQ Sauce)
¼ cup light brown sugar

1. Heat the oil in a large, heavy-bottomed pot or Dutch oven over medium-high heat. Add the ground beef and cook, breaking up the meat with a wooden spoon, until the beef is browned and cooked through, 4–6 minutes. Pour off the grease and return the pot to the heat.

2. Add the bell peppers, scallions, and garlic and cook, stirring occasionally, until the vegetables are softened, about 5 minutes.

3. Add the beans, maple syrup, barbecue sauce, and brown sugar and mix well. Cover the pot, reduce the heat to low, and cook until the sauce has thickened, 15–20 minutes.

CHAPTER 7
Veggies
FOR LIFE

$\mathcal{Y}$OU CAN WALK INTO MY HOUSE, WITH OUR FAMILY OF 11, at any given time and enter a culinary world of diverse dietary lifestyles. We've got carnivores, vegetarians, pescatarians, flexitarians, and plain old picky eaters. You name it, we've got it!

When my kids were younger and I was trying to instill in them the importance of healthy eating, especially eating their vegetables, I introduced them to my dad's roasted cauliflower recipe because it was one of my childhood favorites. Fresh head of cauliflower, seasoned with salt, pepper, dill, and garlic and drizzled with olive oil—simple yet profound. But when I made this dish for my kids, they turned up their noses and said, "This is *OK*, Dad, but can we get some hot wings?" Hot wings?! I knew what needed to be done.

I'm sure you're familiar with the proverb that starts with, "Fool me once, shame on you . . ." Well, my kids got fooled plenty of times, but there was no shame in my game! Before they'd get home from school, I'd chop up a head of cauliflower into bite-size pieces, coat them in seasoned tempura batter, and deep-fry them before tossing them in spicy Buffalo sauce. When it was all said and done, my kids thought they were eating boneless Buffalo chicken bites! This happened a few times before one of them took a closer look and asked me what they were *really* eating. I never lied; I just called them Buffalo bites. Now, a bite of what—that was the question! It all worked out, though, because my kids developed a real love for this dish, and it remains a family favorite to this very day.

Let me help you fool *your* loved ones (or maybe you just come clean) when you prepare my Chunky Buffalo Cauliflower Bites with Vegan Ranch. I hope this dish and the other six Southern-inspired recipes in this chapter leave you with a newfound appreciation for all things veggie. Enjoy!

Chunky Buffalo Cauliflower Bites
with Vegan Ranch | **SERVES 4**

SERVE THIS VEGAN GEM AS a main, side, or appetizer. Its robust flavor is tempered slightly by a cooling, dairy-free ranch dressing with hints of dill. This will surely satisfy those Buffalo chicken cravings as you save on calories, leaving room for dessert—it's all about balance!

Vegetable oil, for frying
1 cup cornstarch
⅔ cup rice flour
1½ teaspoons garlic powder
1 teaspoon smoked paprika
½ teaspoon cayenne pepper
Kosher salt
Cracked black pepper
1 cup plain seltzer
1 head cauliflower, cut into bite-size
    florets
3–4 tablespoons chopped fresh flat-
    leaf parsley, for garnish

Carrots and celery sticks, for
    serving

Vegan Buffalo Sauce
¼ cup plus 2 tablespoons nondairy
    butter
1 teaspoon chili powder
½ teaspoon garlic powder
½ teaspoon onion powder
Pinch cayenne pepper
1¼ cups hot sauce
1–2 tablespoons agave

---

1. Pour vegetable oil into a Dutch oven or large, heavy-bottomed pot to no more than halfway up the side. Prop or clip in a deep-fry thermometer so that the bulb is submerged in the oil. Heat over medium-high heat until the thermometer registers 350 degrees F. (Alternatively, you can use a deep fryer.) Line a plate with paper towels.

2. In a large bowl, whisk together the cornstarch, rice flour, garlic powder, smoked paprika, and cayenne. Season with salt and black pepper as desired.

3. Add the seltzer a little at a time, whisking after each addition, until the batter reaches the right thickness. Not too thick and not too thin—it should coat the back of a spoon without excess dripping.

4. Dip each piece of cauliflower into the batter, tossing to coat evenly.

5. Working in batches, fry the cauliflower until golden brown all over, 7–9 minutes. Remove the cauliflower with a spider and drain on the paper towels.

Southern Inspired

6. While the cauliflower is frying, make the Buffalo sauce. Melt the butter in a medium wok over medium heat. Add the chili powder, garlic powder, onion powder, cayenne, hot sauce, and agave and stir to combine. Bring up to a simmer and cook for 4–5 minutes.

7. Add the fried cauliflower to the sauce in the wok and gently toss to coat evenly. Transfer to a serving dish.

8. Garnish the cauliflower bites with parsley and serve right away with vegan ranch (recipe follows) for dipping and carrots and celery on the side.

Vegan Ranch

1 cup vegan mayonnaise
¼ cup minced fresh dill
1 tablespoon garlic powder
1 tablespoon onion powder
1 teaspoon agave
Kosher salt
Cracked black pepper

1. In a medium bowl, mix together the vegan mayo, dill, garlic powder, onion powder, and agave. Season with salt and pepper to taste.

Savory Arugula Berry Salad | SERVES 4

PEPPERY ARUGULA PAIRED WITH juicy mouthfuls of strawberries, blackberries, and blueberries—garnished with creamy mozzarella and topped with balsamic honey dressing—make this salad a complete meal in itself.

---

4 cups arugula
1 cup sliced strawberries
1 cup sliced blackberries
½ cup blueberries
½ cup fresh mozzarella pieces
⅓ cup walnut halves

⅓ cup balsamic vinegar
½ cup olive oil
2 teaspoons honey
Kosher salt
Cracked black pepper

---

1. Mix the arugula, berries, mozzarella, and walnuts together in a large bowl.

2. In a small bowl, whisk together the balsamic, olive oil, and honey. Pour the dressing over the greens with berries and toss to combine.

3. Season with salt and pepper to taste.

Southern Inspired

Philly Cheese Zucchini Sandwich | SERVES 4

ZUCCHINI IS CLASSIFIED botanically as a fruit but treated like a vegetable in most recipes. Its adaptability lies in its taste, texture, and versatility—and I've called upon all three for this recipe. Enjoy elements of a traditional Philly cheesesteak sandwich—sautéed onions, peppers, mushrooms, and melted provolone—but let zucchini take center stage to give you all the flavor but half the calories!

---

2 tablespoons olive oil
5–6 medium to large zucchini, sliced
    lengthwise ¼ inch thick
½ white onion, sliced
1 green bell pepper, julienned
2 cups thinly sliced button
    mushrooms

Kosher salt
Cracked black pepper
12 slices provolone
Mayonnaise, for serving
4 hoagie rolls, split

---

1. Heat the olive oil in a large skillet over medium-high heat. Sauté the zucchini, onion, bell pepper, and mushrooms until tender, 5–6 minutes. Season with salt and pepper as desired.

2. Place the provolone on top of the vegetables and cover the pan until the steam melts the cheese.

3. Spread mayo on both halves of each roll and divide the cheesy filling into the rolls. Serve right away while hot!

Fried Green Tomatillos | SERVES 4

ALTHOUGH THEY LOOK SIMILAR, tomatillos and tomatoes are different fruits altogether. Tomatillos keep their striking green color as they ripen and tend to be denser and less sweet than tomatoes. Their bright flavor and more acidic bite make them an excellent choice for this recipe when served with sriracha mayo or melted pimento cheese sauce. The key to this dish is double-dredging the sliced tomatillos in the cornmeal batter to enjoy the crispiest crust with each bite—works every time!

Southern Inspired

1½ cups whole milk

2 large eggs

¼ cup hot sauce

1 cup yellow cornmeal

1 cup all-purpose flour

2 tablespoons dried oregano

2 tablespoons garlic powder

2 tablespoons onion powder

1 tablespoon lemon pepper

Kosher salt

Vegetable oil, for frying

8 large tomatillos, sliced ¼–¾ inch thick

Chopped fresh flat-leaf parsley, for garnish (optional)

Sriracha mayonnaise or 1 cup melted pimento cheese, for serving

1. In a large, shallow bowl, whisk together the milk, eggs, and hot sauce. (Start with ¼ cup, but if you want you can add a little more—my momma says one can never have too much hot sauce.)

2. In another large, shallow bowl, whisk together the cornmeal, flour, oregano, garlic powder, onion powder, and lemon pepper and season with salt as desired.

3. Pour vegetable oil into a large, heavy-bottomed pot or Dutch oven no more than halfway up the side. Prop or clip in a deep-fry thermometer so that the bulb is submerged in the oil. Heat over medium-high heat until the thermometer registers 350 degrees F. Line a large plate with paper towels.

4. Dip each tomatillo slice into the milk and hot sauce mixture, then dredge in the flour mixture. Dip again in the milk mixture and then again in the flour mixture.

5. Working in batches, gently lower the battered tomatillos into the hot oil and fry until golden brown, 8–10 minutes. Transfer to the paper towels.

6. Garnish the fried tomatillos with parsley, if you like, and serve with sriracha mayo or melted pimento cheese.

Jackfruit and Rice Stuffed Pineapples | SERVES 4

THE STAR OF THIS VEGAN DISH IS JACKFRUIT. Jackfruit is a fruit that grows in Asia, Africa, and South America—and lucky for us, it can be found in the frozen food or canned goods aisle at your local grocery store. Jackfruit is often treated as a meat substitute—its texture resembles pulled pork, so it can be used in a multitude of ways. The beauty of this dish lies in its Thai barbecue flavor enhanced by fresh pineapple, elegantly served in hollowed-out pineapple "boats." If you don't need this dish to be vegan, you can substitute cooked chicken or shrimp—either way, it's an exotic wonder!

---

2 large ripe pineapples
2 tablespoons avocado oil
1 red bell pepper, small diced
1 green bell pepper, small diced
1 yellow bell pepper, small diced
1½ pounds frozen jackfruit pieces,
    thawed

2 scallions, thinly sliced, plus more
    for garnish
¼ cup your favorite barbecue sauce
    (such as Chef Jernard's Smokey
    Whiskey River Sauce)
¼ cup sweet Thai chili sauce
2 cups cooked jasmine rice

---

1. First, make your pineapple bowls. Split the pineapples down the middle from top to bottom, keeping the stem intact. Hollow out the centers by cutting the pineapple flesh into cross sections or cubes, similar to a tic-tac-toe design. Be careful not to slice through the pineapple rind. With a spoon, carefully scoop the pineapple flesh into a bowl and reserve.

2. Heat the avocado oil in a medium sauté pan over medium-high heat. Sauté the pineapple, bell peppers, jackfruit, and scallions for 3–4 minutes. Add the barbecue sauce and Thai chili sauce and cook, stirring occasionally, until the vegetables have softened, about 7 minutes.

3. Fill the hollowed-out pineapple bowls with equal portions of rice, then scoop the barbecue jackfruit mixture on top. Garnish with more scallions and serve.

Southern Inspired

One-Pot Caribbean Vegetable Noodles | SERVES 4-6

THIS SUPERSTAR VEGAN RECIPE packs a punch of well-being and flavor into each bite. Jackfruit, zucchini noodles, and coconut milk coupled with fresh herbs and curry powder give this quick and easy one-pot wonder serious island vibes—with less mess to clean up!

1–2 tablespoons olive oil
1 medium red onion, small diced
4 garlic cloves, roughly chopped
3 cups canned or frozen jackfruit
   (thawed if frozen)
½ red bell pepper, julienned
½ green bell pepper, julienned
1 cup sliced sun-dried tomatoes,
   optional

Kosher salt
Cracked black pepper
1 (12–16-ounce) can coconut milk
1–1½ tablespoons cornstarch
4 small-medium zucchini, spiralized,
   plus more for garnish
Small bunch fresh thyme, leaves
   stripped, plus more for garnish
1 tablespoon curry powder

---

1. Heat the oil in a large sauté pan over medium-high heat. Add the onion, garlic, and jackfruit and sauté until the onion is tender and the jackfruit is soft, 2–3 minutes.

2. Add the bell peppers and stir to combine, making sure nothing sticks to the bottom. Add the sun-dried tomatoes and drizzle more olive oil over the top. Season with salt and cracked black pepper as desired.

3. Turn up the heat slightly. Add the coconut milk and cornstarch and stir gently to ensure there are no lumps. The cornstarch will begin to thicken as the mixture comes up to a simmer.

4. Reduce the heat to medium and add the zucchini noodles and thyme right over the top. Add the curry powder and cover the pan. Allow the mixture to thicken and the zucchini noodles to cook down for 5–10 minutes. Check a few times to make sure the noodles don't overcook.

5. Serve with more fresh noodles and thyme leaves on top.

BBQ Vegetarian Burger Sliders
with Brussels Sprout Slaw | **SERVES 4**

PLANT-BASED DIETS are becoming more and more popular as people learn about the benefits of this lifestyle and are embracing plant-based "meats" as substitutions for conventional products. I'm not advocating that you mislead your guests, but when you serve these sliders, I bet they won't be able to tell the difference. Let them think the healthy part of the meal lies in the tasty Brussels sprout slaw as they ask for seconds and thirds of these delicious sliders!

Southern Inspired

1 pound ground plant-based meat

6 garlic cloves, roughly chopped

½ cup your favorite barbecue sauce, divided

1 tablespoon olive oil

Kosher salt

Cracked black pepper

8 Hawaiian sweet rolls

Barbecue Seasoning

3 tablespoons garlic powder

3 tablespoons onion powder

2 tablespoons light brown sugar

2 teaspoons smoked paprika

2 teaspoons dried oregano

Brussels Sprout Slaw

1 cup mayonnaise

1 tablespoon yellow mustard

1 tablespoon sweet pickle relish

2 cups thinly shaved Brussels sprouts

2 medium carrots, thinly shaved

1. In a medium bowl, mix together the plant-based meat and garlic.

2. In a small bowl, whisk together all the ingredients for the barbecue seasoning.

3. Add half of the seasoning mixture to the meat and garlic (save the rest for the slaw). Then add half of the barbecue sauce. Mix everything together until the seasonings and sauce are well incorporated into the meat. Form the meat mixture into eight mini patties.

4. Set a rack in a rimmed baking sheet. Heat the olive oil on a griddle over high heat. Add the patties and cook until golden brown, 3–4 minutes per side. Set them aside on the rack to rest and sprinkle with a little salt and pepper.

5. To make the Brussels sprout slaw, in a large bowl, whisk together the mayo, mustard, and relish. Add the Brussels sprouts and carrots and sprinkle with a few pinches of the remaining barbecue seasoning.

6. To assemble the sliders, place a patty on each bun. Top with some of the slaw and a drizzle of the remaining barbecue sauce.

CHAPTER 8
Wings
AND THINGS

*M*Y WIFE AND I LOVE US SOME CANDY APPLES! IN FACT, Keena loves them so much that she was the inspiration behind my Candy Apple Wings—well, her and my love for carnival food.

Growing up in Mississippi, I couldn't wait for the carnivals to come through town. The rides, games, and shows were the big draw for most, but I went for the food more than anything else. Walking through those stalls you were wrapped in whiffs of cotton candy, roasted corn, deep-fried *everything*, smoked turkey legs—and of course my favorite, candy apples. You can't find those collective smells anywhere *but* at a carnival! I was hypnotized by those super shiny, almost stained glass-like, cherry-red candy orbs. I'd take my first bite—sugary crackle crunch contrasted against the tanginess of the apple. For a moment I'd forget that I was surrounded by bumper cars, carousels, and roller-coasters and fall under its spell.

As the years passed and I developed my palate as a chef, I learned that the beauty of most complex flavors lies in the contrast or blending of flavors to achieve richer taste profiles. I drew upon this understanding as I created my Candy Apple Wings recipe. Here, I want you to experience the nostalgia of this sweet treat as it glazes a smoky, spicy wing. I kid you not—you'll be reminded of candy apples each time you take a bite! Think of the dishes throughout this chapter as perfect conversation starters at your next party or get-together—"wings" four different ways and "things" like Chicken Cheeseburger Egg Rolls, Creamy Collard Green Dip, and Tempura-Battered Green Beans will keep your guests mixing and mingling. This is what you want!

Candy Apple Wings | SERVES 4–5

THESE SHINY RED, GLISTENING WINGS are easy on the eyes and heavenly on the tongue. They're equal parts sugared smokiness and fiery crunch. Whether deep-fried, air-fried, baked, or grilled—and topped with blue cheese crumbles—these juicy crimson chicken wings will kick things off with a bang!

Southern Inspired

Vegetable oil, for frying

2 pounds chicken wings, separated into drumettes and flats (wing tips discarded)

Kosher salt

Cracked black pepper

Blue cheese crumbles, for garnish

Candy Apple Sauce

¼ cup packed dark brown sugar

2 tablespoons unsalted butter

1 tablespoon chili powder

1 teaspoon garlic powder

1 teaspoon cayenne pepper

1 cup apple whiskey

1 cup your favorite hot sauce

½ cup cherry cola

¼ cup grenadine

1 tablespoon honey

1. In a small pot or skillet, combine all the ingredients for the candy apple sauce. Stir the ingredients together over medium-low heat and bring to a simmer. Cook until the sauce thickens, 10–15 minutes. Remove the sauce from the heat.

2. Pour oil into a large Dutch oven or heavy-bottomed pot to no more than halfway up the side. Prop or clip in a deep-fry thermometer so that the bulb is submerged in the oil. Heat over medium-high heat until the thermometer registers 350 degrees F. (Alternatively, you can use a deep fryer or air fryer.) Line a platter with paper towels (or set a rack in a rimmed baking sheet).

3. Season the wings with salt and pepper. Working in batches to not crowd the pot, gently drop the wings into the hot oil. Fry until the wings are golden brown and cooked through, 10–15 minutes. Transfer to the paper towels or rack.

4. Pour some of the sauce into a large bowl and toss with some of the wings until they are evenly coated. Working in batches makes it easier to coat them evenly. As a general rule, toss about 10 wings per ¾ cup sauce.

5. Arrange the coated wings on a platter and garnish with blue cheese crumbles.

Chicken Cheeseburger Egg Rolls | SERVES 8–10

THESE ARE A *BIG* HIT with my kids and their friends. I think it's the crunch of the egg roll wrapper, the welcome surprise of the cheeseburger filling, and the tanginess of the sweet and spicy chili mayo dipping sauce that make this fusion snack a favorite. If you'd prefer not to deep-fry these egg rolls, try air-frying them according to the manufacturer's instructions.

1–2 tablespoons olive oil
1 small yellow onion, minced
1 pound ground chicken
Kosher salt
Cracked black pepper
½ cup shredded cheddar cheese
¼ cup shredded provolone cheese
¼ cup diced bread and butter
    pickles
1 large egg white

1 tablespoon water
8–10 egg roll wrappers
Vegetable oil, for frying
Sliced scallions, for garnish

Chili Mayo Dipping Sauce
½ cup chili sauce
½ cup mayonnaise
Juice of 1 small lime

1. Coat a large skillet with olive oil and heat over medium heat. Add the onion and sweat until translucent and soft, 2–3 minutes.

2. Add the ground chicken and cook, using a wooden spoon to break up the meat. Season with salt and pepper as desired. Build those flavors!

3. Add the cheeses and pickles and stir into the ground chicken mixture. Once the chicken has cooked through and the cheese has melted, transfer the mixture to a large bowl and allow to cool slightly. You can cover the bowl and chill it in the fridge until you're ready to proceed.

4. Make an egg wash by whisking the egg white and water in a small bowl.

5. Once the mixture has cooled enough to handle, lay one egg roll wrapper on a work surface so that one corner is pointing toward you. Spoon about 2 tablespoons of the chicken mixture into the center of one egg roll wrapper. (Don't use more—overfilling makes them hard to roll!) Brush the outer edges of the wrapper with some egg wash. Fold the corner closest to you to the opposite corner so the wrapper forms a triangle shape. Fold over both the left and right corners and pull them into the center of the roll. Then tuck and roll until the roll is completely sealed. Continue with the remaining filling and egg roll wrappers.

6. Pour vegetable oil into a large Dutch oven or heavy-bottomed pot to no more than halfway up the side. Prop or clip in a deep-fry thermometer so that the bulb is submerged in the oil. Heat over medium-high heat until the thermometer registers 350 degrees F. Line a platter with paper towels (or set a rack in a rimmed baking sheet).

7. Gently drop a few egg rolls into the hot oil. Fry until golden brown and crispy, about 4 minutes. Repeat until all the egg rolls are cooked. Transfer the cooked egg rolls to the paper towels or rack.

8. While the egg rolls are frying, in a medium bowl, whisk together all the ingredients for the chili mayo dipping sauce.

9. Arrange the egg rolls on a serving platter and garnish with scallions. Serve with the dipping sauce.

Roasted Coconut Hot Wings | SERVES 8–10

CAN'T GET AWAY TO A TROPICAL PARADISE for some much-needed R & R? No problem. Let these hot wings take you beachside as you enjoy their spicy coconut crunch. Serve them with my Tempura-Battered Green Beans with Wasabi Mayo Dipping Sauce and your favorite beverage for some island hopping of your very own.

4–5 pounds chicken wings,
    separated into drumettes and
    flats (wing tips discarded)
Kosher salt
Cracked black pepper
½ cup coconut flakes, divided
¼ cup canned coconut milk

½ cup your favorite hot sauce
3 tablespoons coconut sugar
1 tablespoon cayenne pepper
1 tablespoon chili powder
Minced fresh flat-leaf parsley, for
    garnish

---

1. Preheat the oven to 375 degrees F. Line a rimmed baking sheet with parchment paper.

2. Season the wings with salt, pepper, and a sprinkle of coconut flakes (save some for later). Arrange the wings on the lined baking sheet in a single layer.

3. Bake for 45–55 minutes, until the wings are golden and crispy. Place them on paper towels to drain.

4. Heat the coconut milk in a wok or a large saucepan over medium heat. Add the hot sauce, coconut sugar, cayenne pepper, and chili powder. Bring to a low simmer and cook until the sauce thickens, about 10 minutes.

5. Toss the chicken wings in the wok with the sauce until they're completely coated.

6. Transfer the wings to a serving platter. Garnish with the remaining coconut flakes and minced parsley.

Southern Inspired

"Oh Yeah" Golden Honey Hot Wings | SERVES 8–10

THESE PARTY WINGS PACK A POWERHOUSE of flavor—heat, sweet, tart, and tangy! Pairing them with my Creamy Collard Green Dip and Crostini and Get Your Life Right Party Punch will make this an "Oh Yeah, Baby Baby" trio!

Vegetable oil, for frying
4–5 pounds chicken wings,
    separated into drumettes and
    flats (wing tips discarded)
Kosher salt
Cracked black pepper

"Oh Yeah" Sauce
¾ cup honey
½ cup water
½ cup yellow mustard
¼ cup your favorite hot sauce
1 tablespoon smoked paprika
1 tablespoon garlic powder
1 tablespoon onion powder
2 teaspoons cayenne pepper

1. Bring all the sauce ingredients to a simmer in a wok over medium-high heat. Remove from the heat and set aside.

2. Pour vegetable oil into a large Dutch oven or heavy-bottomed pot to no more than halfway up the side. Prop or clip in a deep-fry thermometer so that the bulb is submerged in the oil. Heat over medium-high heat until the thermometer registers 350 degrees F. (Alternatively, you can use a deep fryer or air fryer.) Line a platter with paper towels (or set a rack in a rimmed baking sheet).

3. Season the wings with salt and pepper. Working in batches to not crowd the pot, gently drop the wings into the hot oil. Fry until the wings are golden brown and cooked through, 10–15 minutes. Transfer to the paper towels or rack.

4. Toss the wings in the wok with the sauce until evenly coated. Serve right away.

Creamy Collard Green Dip and Crostini | SERVES 4-6

THIS FAMILY CLASSIC GRACES OUR TABLE at every New Year's Eve party. It's a Southern custom to eat collard greens in the new year to welcome prosperity into your life—and this dip, with its creamy earthiness, helps keep this tradition alive in our home. But feel free to make this anytime, because what's a party without a tasty dip?

Southern Inspired

Olive oil

2 small bunches collard greens, stemmed and chopped

½ red bell pepper, julienned

1 small yellow onion, small diced

3 tablespoons unsalted butter

3 tablespoons all-purpose flour

1 cup heavy cream

1 teaspoon chopped fresh dill

1 teaspoon minced fresh flat-leaf parsley

Kosher salt

Cracked black pepper

¾ cup sour cream

½ cup mayonnaise

½ teaspoon garlic powder

½ teaspoon onion powder

Grated Parmesan cheese, for serving (optional)

Crostini

1 baguette, cut into ½-inch slices

¼ cup olive oil

1 tablespoon minced fresh flat-leaf parsley

1. Preheat the oven to 400 degrees F.

2. Heat a drizzle of olive oil in a large sauté pan over medium-high heat. Add the collard greens and cook for a few minutes until they begin to wilt, then add the bell pepper and cook for 1–2 minutes. Add the onion and continue to cook until the pepper and onion are soft and the onion is translucent, about 5 minutes.

3. Add the butter and let it melt into the vegetables. Stir the flour into the butter and vegetables and cook for a few minutes.

4. Stream in the heavy cream, stirring or whisking all the while. Simmer for a few minutes until the cream reduces slightly.

5. Add the dill and parsley and season with salt and pepper to taste.

6. Reduce the heat to low and fold in the sour cream and mayo. Stir in the garlic powder and onion powder. Cook over medium-low heat until the sauce has reduced a bit and the mixture is creamy, about 5 minutes.

7. In the meantime, arrange the slices of bread in a single layer on a rack set in a large baking sheet. Drizzle or brush each side with olive oil. Sprinkle fresh parsley on top and bake for 6–8 minutes or until lightly golden. Keep an eye on them because they will cook quickly!

8. Sprinkle grated Parmesan over the top of the dip and serve with crostini for dipping.

Tempura-Battered Green Beans
with Wasabi Mayo Dipping Sauce | **SERVES 4–6**

THESE GREEN BEANS MAINTAIN their vibrancy and crunch after a light coating of tempura batter and a quick frying before partnering with a pungent yet cooling wasabi dipping sauce. If you don't have tempura batter mix on hand, try substituting rice flour for similar results.

2 cups tempura batter mix
1 tablespoon garlic powder
1 tablespoon onion powder
½ teaspoon smoked paprika
1–2 cups plain seltzer water
Kosher salt
Cracked black pepper

1 pound green beans
Vegetable oil, for frying
1 cup mayonnaise
1 tablespoon wasabi
1–2 tablespoons canned coconut milk
Black sesame seeds, for garnish

1. In a large bowl, combine the tempura batter mix, garlic and onion powders, and smoked paprika. Slowly whisk in the seltzer until the batter reaches your desired consistency. Not too thin or too thick—it should look similar to pancake batter. Season with salt and pepper.

2. Add the green beans and toss to coat evenly.

3. Pour vegetable oil into a large, heavy-bottomed pot or Dutch oven to no more than halfway up the side. Prop or clip in a deep-fry thermometer so that the bulb is submerged in the oil. Heat over medium-high heat until the thermometer registers 350 degrees F. Line a plate with paper towels.

4. Fry the green beans until they crisp up and turn golden brown, 5–7 minutes. Transfer to the paper towels.

5. While the beans are frying, in a medium bowl, mix together the mayo, wasabi, and coconut milk. Sprinkle the mixture with black sesame seeds.

6. Serve the green beans with the wasabi mayo dipping sauce.

Tipsy Tequila Wings | SERVES 4–6

WITH NOTES OF TEQUILA, pineapple, honey, and chipotle peppers, these saucy oven-baked wings will warm your palate as you enjoy their satisfying bite. I like the combination of mild, mineral-rich Himalayan salt with the tequila, but you can use kosher salt or sea salt instead. Why not go all the way and pair these lip-smackers with my Citrusy Lime Margarita for a fiesta of your very own!

½ cup cornstarch
3 tablespoons lemon pepper, plus
    more for garnish
2 tablespoons garlic powder
2 tablespoons onion powder
2 teaspoons smoked paprika
2 pounds chicken wings, separated
    into drumettes and flats (wing
    tips discarded)
Himalayan Salt
Chopped fresh flat-leaf parsley, for
    garnish

Tipsy Tequila Sauce
¼ cup canned chipotles in adobo,
    chopped
2 tablespoons minced garlic
¼ teaspoon Himalayan salt
½ cup tequila
½ cup honey
½ cup pineapple juice

1. Preheat the oven to 375 degrees F. Line a rimmed baking sheet with aluminum foil.

2. In a medium saucepan, combine all the sauce ingredients and bring to a low simmer over medium-high heat. Cook, stirring constantly, until the sauce has reduced and thickened, 8–10 minutes. Remove from the heat and allow the sauce to cool slightly.

3. In a large bowl, mix the cornstarch, lemon pepper, garlic powder, onion powder, smoked paprika, and salt as desired. Toss the wings in the seasoning coating evenly.

4. Arrange the wings in a single layer on the lined baking sheet. Bake for 45–50 minutes or until the wings are lightly golden brown and cooked through. Place them on paper towels to drain.

Southern Inspired

5. Transfer the wings to a large bowl. Pour the sauce over the wings and toss to coat.

6. Arrange the wings on a serving platter. Garnish with parsley and a sprinkle of lemon pepper.

CHAPTER 9

ON THE
Side

*L*ET'S TALK ABOUT CORN BREAD—NOT WHAT COMES OUT OF that blue-and-white box so many of us know, but homemade corn bread as a staple of American cuisine. There's the Northern version that leans sweeter, and there's the more savory buttermilk-based Southern style. Either one can usually be found on dinner tables during Thanksgiving, as a side dish at any number of restaurants, or as a daily fixings item on plates across the country. Corn bread is even more American than apple pie since it was Native Americans who introduced this specialty to European settlers as they explored the New World—well before the establishment of the first colony at Jamestown in 1607.

At one point when I was growing up, my siblings came home from their friends' houses and told my mom that they didn't like the corn bread that she and my great-grandmother used to make. They had tasted the contents of that blue-and-white box and wanted *that* instead. Sacrilege! Gwen didn't miss a beat: "Don't bring that boxed stuff in here!" She pulled out a Bundt pan and some fresh honey and got to modifying her tried-and-true recipe—transforming it into a sweeter buttermilk-based corn bread, cut and served like a slice of cake. My corn bread prodigal siblings returned home!

When I was younger and saw my mother or great-grandmother making corn bread, I knew what was coming—collard greens with smoked turkey legs, pinto beans, or black-eyed peas. As I would dish up my plate, my great-grandmother, Lil Momma, would always say, "Baby, you better make sure you get a big slice of that corn bread to suck up that pot liquor (also spelled potlikker), cause that's where all the flavor is!" She sure had a way with words.

All eight side dishes in this chapter will help shine a Southern spotlight on whatever spread you're planning. As for my Mini Corn Bread recipe, don't forget to cut the slices big enough to suck up *your* pot liquor!

Mini Corn Bread | MAKES 2 MINI BUNDTS; SERVES 6-8

THIS BUTTERMILK CORN BREAD packs a punch with the addition of minced habanero and cracked black pepper. Baked to a golden brown and drizzled with honey, this balanced side dish may very well steal the show!

---

2 cups cornmeal
1 cup all-purpose flour
3 tablespoons sugar
1½ teaspoons salt
¼ teaspoon cracked black pepper
2 large eggs
2 cups buttermilk

½ cup whole milk
1 cup (2 sticks) unsalted butter, melted
1 red habanero, minced
Honey, for serving
¼ cup sliced scallions, for garnish

---

1. Preheat the oven to 350 degrees F.

2. Grease two 6½-inch nonstick mini Bundt pans or mini cast iron skillets.

3. In a medium bowl, whisk together the cornmeal, flour, sugar, salt, and pepper. In another medium bowl, whisk together the eggs, buttermilk, whole milk, butter, and habanero. Add the wet ingredients to the dry and thoroughly combine. The batter should have a thick consistency similar to that of pancake batter.

4. Pour the batter into the prepared pans. Bake for 25–30 minutes or until a toothpick inserted in the center comes out clean.

5. Serve with a drizzle of honey and garnish with scallions, if desired.

Cavatappi Pasta Salad | SERVES 4-6

CAVATAPPI IS AN S-SHAPED PASTA that looks like hollow corkscrews. (In fact, the word *cavatappi* means corkscrew in Italian.) It holds sauces and dressings very well, which is why it makes for an excellent base in this delicious salad.

Kosher salt

1 pound cavatappi pasta

1 cup mayonnaise

2 tablespoons apple cider vinegar

1½–2 tablespoons sugar

1 tablespoon dry mustard

1 teaspoon smoked paprika

1 teaspoon chopped fresh dill

Cracked black pepper

1 red onion, small diced

1 red bell pepper, medium diced

1 green bell pepper, medium diced

2 medium carrots, julienned

2 large celery ribs, small diced

1 cup small broccoli florets

---

1. Bring a large pot of salted water to a boil. Cook the pasta according to the package directions until al dente. Drain and set aside to cool completely.

2. In a large bowl, whisk together the mayonnaise, vinegar, sugar, dry mustard, smoked paprika, fresh dill, and salt and pepper to taste.

3. Add the pasta to the dressing and toss to coat well. Fold in the red onion, bell peppers, carrots, celery, and broccoli. Season with salt and pepper to taste, cover, and chill until ready to serve.

Southern Inspired

Cajun Sweet Potato Fries | SERVES 4–6

THESE BOLD SWEET POTATO FRIES make a great partner for "The Big Juicy" Smoked Gouda Cheeseburger, Crab Cake Texas Toast Burger, or Philly Cheese Zucchini Sandwich. To keep these fries crunchy, remember to fry them in small batches to avoid overcrowding in the pot—nobody likes a soggy fry.

Vegetable oil, for frying

¼ cup Cajun seasoning, homemade (page 20) or store-bought

3 tablespoons light brown sugar

Kosher salt

4 sweet potatoes, peeled and cut into ½-inch-thick fries

Chopped scallions, for garnish

1 lemon, cut into wedges (optional)

Ketchup, for serving

---

1. Pour oil into a large Dutch oven or heavy-bottomed pot to no more than halfway up the side. Prop or clip in a deep-fry thermometer so that the bulb is submerged in the oil. Heat over medium-high heat until the thermometer registers 350 degrees F.

2. In a large bowl, combine the Cajun seasoning, brown sugar, and salt as desired. Set aside.

3. Working in batches to not crowd the pot, fry the potatoes until golden brown and crispy, 10–12 minutes. As the fries come out of the oil, toss them in the seasoning mixture, then transfer to a plate.

4. Garnish with scallions and add a squeeze of lemon juice if you like. Serve with ketchup on the side for dipping.

Zesty Coleslaw | SERVES 4–6

THERE ARE SUBTLE DIFFERENCES between good coleslaw and *great* coleslaw, and I'd like to think this recipe is the latter. It starts with green and red cabbage to give crunch, color, and character. Then it builds upon flavors of creamy, sweet, tangy, and slightly savory with mayonnaise, sweet pickle relish, a bit of sugar, apple cider vinegar, and herbaceous celery salt to make a superb dressing. And there you have it—a *great* slaw.

½ medium head green cabbage, shredded

½ medium head red cabbage, shredded

½ cup mayonnaise

¼ cup yellow mustard

¼ cup sweet pickle relish

3 tablespoons sugar

2 tablespoons celery salt

2 tablespoons apple cider vinegar

Kosher salt

Cracked black pepper

---

1. In a large bowl, toss the cabbage with the mayonnaise and mustard until well combined.

2. Add the relish, sugar, celery salt, and vinegar and season with salt and pepper as desired. Mix all the ingredients until thoroughly combined.

3. Cover and refrigerate to set up for about 30 minutes before serving, or enjoy the next day.

Southern Inspired

Cheesy Wilted Spinach | SERVES 4-6

THE KEY TO THIS DISH IS cooking the spinach just long enough for it to shrink and turn a beautiful bright green. Keep an eye on the time to avoid it turning mushy and bitter.

---

2 tablespoons olive oil
2 tablespoons minced garlic
1-1½ pounds spinach, stemmed
¼ cup vegetable or chicken broth

Kosher salt
Cracked black pepper
½ cup grated Parmesan cheese

---

1. Heat the olive oil in a large sauté pan over medium-high heat. Add the garlic and sauté until lightly golden, 2–3 minutes.

2. Dump the spinach on top and stir into the garlic. Add the broth and season with salt and pepper as desired. Reduce the heat to medium and cook until the spinach has wilted, 3–5 minutes.

3. Remove the pan from the heat. Fold in the Parmesan cheese and serve hot.

Sautéed Cabbage with Turkey Bacon | SERVES 4-6

CABBAGE IS SO VERSATILE and common to many cuisines. Easy to grow in various climates and simple to prepare, cabbage can be dressed up or down to act like a main, side, or garnish. Here, I call upon memories of my great-grandmother, Lil Momma, as I channel her recipe for sautéed cabbage. Savory, bright, and full of kick, this dish would pair well with my Jerk Beef Ribs or My Dad's Oxtails with Momma's Buttery Garlic Whipped Potatoes.

---

2 tablespoons olive oil
8 ounces turkey bacon, cut into
 ½ inch pieces
1 medium yellow onion, diced
½ head medium green cabbage,
 shredded
½ head medium red cabbage,
 shredded

1 large garlic clove, minced
1 teaspoon crushed red pepper
1 teaspoon onion powder
1 teaspoon garlic powder
Kosher salt
Cracked black pepper

---

1. Heat the olive oil in a large skillet over medium-high heat. Add the turkey bacon and cook until golden brown, about 3–5 minutes.

2. Add the onion and sauté until translucent, 3–4 minutes. Add the cabbage and garlic and stir into the onion and bacon.

3. While the cabbage begins to wilt, add the crushed red pepper, onion powder, and garlic powder and season with salt and pepper as desired.

4. Sauté the mixture until the cabbage is tender, 6–8 minutes.

Southern Inspired

Cast Iron Skillet Creamed Corn | SERVES 4–6

WE USED TO KICK OFF THE WEEKEND on *Thursday* nights in my house when I was growing up. Having my mom's creamed corn and grilled pork chops for dinner signaled the good times had begun. Just like Gwen, I use a cast iron skillet to prepare this sweet and velvety side dish. If you're feeling ambitious, use a corn peeler or sharp knife to remove the kernels from fresh cobs; otherwise, frozen corn will do just fine.

5 tablespoons unsalted butter, divided	¼ cup sugar
1 small onion, small diced	Kosher salt
1 red bell pepper, small diced	Cracked black pepper
1½ cups fresh or frozen white corn kernels (thawed if frozen)	¼ cup all-purpose flour
	¼ cup vegetable broth
1½ cups fresh or frozen yellow corn kernels (thawed if frozen)	2 cups heavy cream
	1 bunch scallions, chopped, for garnish

1. Melt 2 tablespoons of the butter in a large skillet over medium-high heat. Add the onion, bell pepper, and corn and sauté until the vegetables soften and turn lightly golden brown, 6–8 minutes. Stir in the sugar and season with salt and pepper as desired.

2. Melt the remaining 3 tablespoons butter into the vegetables. Whisk in the flour so it begins to coat the vegetables. Cook, stirring, for about 2–3 minutes so the raw flour taste cooks out. It may begin to look pasty in texture.

3. Whisk in the broth, making sure there are no clumps. Stir in the heavy cream and cook over medium heat until the cream has reduced and thickened, about 10 minutes.

4. Garnish the skillet corn with scallions just before serving.

Sautéed Asparagus | SERVES 4

ASPARAGUS IS A UNIQUELY FLAVORED, nutritious vegetable. It has been described as strong, bitter, grassy, and broccoli-like—perhaps hard to pin down but easy to enjoy. Sautéing asparagus with minced garlic and shallot will temper any bitter undertones and leave you with a more delicate flavor.

---

2 tablespoons avocado oil
1 bunch asparagus, ends trimmed
1 tablespoon minced garlic

2–3 teaspoons minced shallot
Kosher salt
Cracked black pepper

---

1. Heat the avocado oil in a large sauté pan over medium-high heat. Add the asparagus in a single layer and cook for 2 minutes.

2. Add the garlic and shallot and season with salt and pepper as desired. Continue to cook undisturbed until the asparagus is tender, 2–3 minutes.

CHAPTER 10
Brunch

*W*HEN I WAS GROWING UP, WE ENJOYED *SATURDAY* brunch because Sundays were reserved for hours-long church services—and every Saturday that table was full of our favorites: BBQ Shrimp and Grits, Deviled Eggs, Chicken and Waffles, and, of course, Kale and Shrimp Salad. Our brunches tended to be neighborhood affairs because brunch is meant to be shared—we couldn't keep all that goodness to ourselves!

A little over 10 years ago, kale reached celebrity status. Kale was on the cover of magazines, featured in recipes on cooking shows, plastered across T-shirts—it was even served at the Super Bowl! Kale was having its moment. And rightfully so: it's tasty, it can be eaten in a variety of ways, it's extremely nutritious, and it's low in calories. I'm not new to the kale game. In fact, me and kale go way, way back—back to my childhood Saturday brunch table. However, I'm an honest man and I can't deny that my beloved green can be somewhat *resistant* and bitter. But my great-grandmother, Lil Momma, had a solution for that. Massage. Yes, massaging that kale!

You might have seen a video or two showing you how to soften the stubborn leaves of this cabbage cousin by adding a dash of salt and maybe some lemon juice before massaging it for a few minutes. But Lil Momma had been massaging kale for decades before these tutorials showed up. It was a familiar sight to see her sitting on the porch or walking through the house with her sealed plastic bags filled with kale, a pinch of salt and a slight drizzle of olive oil—gently massaging, never breaking its spirit, merely tempering its toughness before adding it to salad. The process seemed almost meditative for her.

As you break bread with friends and family during the weekend, I hope you'll enjoy my many brunch-worthy dishes from this chapter. When you serve my Kale and Shrimp Salad with Warm Cranberry Dressing, be sure to show that kale some love by giving it a little massage—you can thank me later.

BBQ Shrimp and Grits | SERVES 4-6

WHEN I WAS GROWING UP, brunch wouldn't have been brunch without friends, family, *and* shrimp and grits! I've kept this dish lively by adding some Cajun heat and whiskey barbecue sauce. Don't have whiskey barbecue sauce on hand? No problem—just add a dash of whiskey to your favorite barbecue sauce and enjoy!

Smoked Cheddar Grits

3 cups no-sodium chicken broth

1 tablespoon unsalted butter

1 cup quick grits

1 cup shredded smoked cheddar cheese, plus more for garnish

Kosher salt

BBQ Shrimp

1 teaspoon olive oil

2 tablespoons unsalted butter

½ green bell pepper, medium diced

½ red bell pepper, medium diced

1 small Vidalia onion, small diced

Kosher salt

Cracked black pepper

1–2 links of your favorite barbecue sausage, sliced

1 pound jumbo shrimp, peeled (tails left on) and deveined

1½ teaspoons smoked paprika

1½ teaspoons Cajun seasoning, homemade (page 20) or store-bought

1 cup smoky whiskey barbecue sauce

Sliced scallions, for garnish

1. First, make the grits so they are ready once your shrimp are done. In a medium saucepan, bring the chicken broth and butter to a boil over medium-high heat. Add the grits in a steady stream and whisk quickly. Turn the heat down to medium-low and cook the grits until tender and creamy, 7–8 minutes. Add more liquid if needed to achieve the desired consistency. Fold in the smoked cheddar cheese and season with salt to taste.

2. While the grits are cooking, make the shrimp. Melt together the olive oil and butter over medium-high heat. Add the bell peppers and onion and sauté until soft, about 5 minutes. Season with salt and pepper as desired. Add the sausage and stir to combine.

3. Season the shrimp on each side with the smoked paprika and Cajun seasoning. Make room in the pan to add the shrimp and nestle them into the peppers, onion, and sausage mixture. Cook the shrimp for 4–6 minutes, then flip them, add the barbecue sauce, and continue cooking until the shrimp are pink and tender, 1–2 minutes more.

4. Divide the grits between bowls. Spoon the barbecue shrimp and sausage sauce over top. Garnish with more cheese and scallions and serve.

Peach Chicken and Waffles | SERVES 4–6

BRING ON THE PEACHES *AND* THE HOT SAUCE, because this brunch celebrity has arrived! These well-seasoned chicken wings grace the tops of light and crispy peach waffles and are lovingly bathed in a spicy, peach-infused maple syrup. The secret ingredient for fluffy waffles is seltzer water. The secret ingredient for scrumptious wings is love!

Fried Chicken Wings
Vegetable oil, for frying
2 pounds whole chicken wings
Kosher salt
Cracked black pepper
3 cups all-purpose flour
1 tablespoon cayenne pepper
1 tablespoon smoked paprika
1 tablespoon dried oregano
1 tablespoon onion powder
1 tablespoon garlic powder
1 cup whole milk
1 cup water
1 large egg

Waffles
1¼ cups cake flour
1¼ cups all purpose flour
¼ cup sugar

1½ teaspoons baking powder
1 teaspoon baking soda
½ teaspoon salt
Pinch ground allspice
2 large eggs, room temperature
8 tablespoons (1 stick) unsalted
    butter, melted and cooled to
    room temperature
½ teaspoon vanilla extract
1 cup club soda or seltzer
¼ cup whole milk
¼ cup canned peach syrup
Sliced fresh or canned peaches, for
    serving (optional)

Peach-Maple Hot Sauce
1 cup canned peach syrup
½ cup pure maple syrup
½ cup your favorite hot sauce

1. Pour vegetable oil into a large cast iron skillet to no more than halfway up the side. Prop or clip in a deep-fry thermometer so that the bulb is submerged in the oil. Heat over medium-high heat until the thermometer registers 350 degrees F. Set a rack in a rimmed baking sheet.

2. Season the chicken wings with salt and pepper in a large bowl and turn to coat. In another large bowl, whisk together the flour and spices and season with salt and pepper.

(continued)

3. In a third large bowl, whisk together the milk, water, and egg.

4. Here comes the fun part: double-breading your chicken wings. Dip the chicken wings into the liquid mixture, then dredge in the dry mixture, then back into the liquid, and finish with another coating of dry mixture.

5. Working in batches to not crowd the pot, drop the wings into the hot oil and fry until they are golden brown, crispy, and cooked through, 15–20 minutes. Transfer the chicken to the rack.

6. To make the waffle batter, in a large bowl, whisk together the cake flour, all-purpose flour, sugar, baking powder, baking soda, salt, and allspice. In a separate large bowl, whisk together the eggs and butter, then add the vanilla extract.

7. Pour the butter and egg mixture into the dry ingredients and mix well. Slowly stream in the club soda, milk, and peach syrup. Whisk until the batter is smooth with minimal lumps.

8. Grease your waffle iron and preheat it. Pour a bit of the batter into the center of the iron (how much depends on the size of your waffle iron!) and close. Cook until the waffle is lightly golden, 3–4 minutes. (If you want a darker, stiffer waffle, cook longer.) Repeat with the remaining batter. The batter should make about 5 standard waffles.

9. In the meantime, make the sauce for the chicken and waffles. In a small saucepan, combine the peach syrup, maple syrup, and hot sauce. Bring the mixture to a simmer over medium heat and cook until it reduces into a thick syrup, 3–5 minutes.

10. Plate a few pieces of chicken on top of your waffles and drizzle with the peach-maple hot sauce. If you like, garnish each plate with a few slices of peach.

Southern Inspired

Muddled Strawberry Lemonade | SERVES 6

SOMEHOW A MUDDLED DRINK SEEMS FANCY, but there's more to it than that. Muddling helps release the fresh flavors of your fruit into your beverage, making it tastier. Prepare this recipe with homemade lemonade or store-bought—either way, this drink is perfect any time of year.

2 cups hulled strawberries	**3 quarts your favorite strawberry**
Large ice cubes	**lemonade**
	¼ cup fresh mint leaves

1. Muddle the strawberries in the bottom of a large pitcher until mashed into small pieces.

2. Add the ice and pour over the lemonade. Top with fresh mint and serve right away.

Kale and Shrimp Salad with Warm Cranberry Dressing | SERVES 4

I USED TO WATCH MY GREAT-GRANDMOTHER, Lil Momma, massage kale before adding it to the salad bowl—knowing that its softened texture would make for a pleasant base—and waited in anticipation for it to be served with shrimp and her homemade barbecue sauce. I looked forward to brunch *every* week! This version bathes the salad in a warm honey-balsamic dressing and finishes it with full-flavored Gorgonzola crumbles for my take on a family favorite.

Southern Inspired

1 bunch curly kale, trimmed and
thinly sliced
16 ounces baby kale
5 tablespoons olive oil, divided
Kosher salt
Cracked black pepper
1 shallot, minced
3 garlic cloves, roughly chopped
8 ounces jumbo shrimp, peeled (tails
left on) and deveined

1 teaspoon smoked paprika
¾ cup dried cranberries
¼ cup balsamic vinegar
1 tablespoon honey
⅓ cup chopped walnuts
Grated zest and juice of 1 lemon
½ cup crumbled Gorgonzola cheese,
optional

1. Put the kale in a large resealable plastic bag. Add 3 tablespoons of the olive oil, season with salt and pepper as desired, and seal the bag, pressing out as much air as possible. Massage the kale vigorously until the kale starts to break down and soften, 5–10 minutes.

2. In a large skillet, heat the remaining 2 tablespoons olive oil over medium-high heat. Sauté the shallot and garlic until the shallot is translucent, 1–2 minutes.

3. In a medium bowl, toss the shrimp with the smoked paprika and season with salt and pepper as desired.

4. Add the shrimp to the pan in a single layer and cook until opaque and pink, 2–3 minutes per side.

5. Add the cranberries, balsamic vinegar, and honey. Bring up to a simmer and cook until the sauce thickens to a syrupy consistency.

6. Remove the pan from the heat and set aside to cool slightly.

7. Transfer the kale to a large serving bowl. Pour on the shrimp and warm dressing. Add the walnuts, lemon zest and juice, and crumbled Gorgonzola. Toss gently to combine and serve right away.

Southern-Style Deviled Eggs with Bacon Crumbles | SERVES 4–6

SOUTHERN-STYLE DEVILED EGGS usually include sweet pickle relish and yellow mustard and are garnished with a sprinkling of paprika. I've pretty much kept this recipe traditional, except for the addition of turkey bacon crumbles as a finishing touch. If you prefer a more savory version, try swapping dill pickle relish for sweet.

Kosher salt
6–8 large eggs
¼ cup mayonnaise
2 tablespoons sweet pickle relish
2 tablespoons yellow mustard
1 tablespoon light brown sugar

1 teaspoon smoked paprika, plus
  more for garnish
½ teaspoon garlic powder
Cracked black pepper
¼ cup cooked and crumbled turkey
  bacon

---

1. Bring a medium pot of salted water to a boil. Fill a large bowl with cold water and ice cubes. Add the eggs to the pot and boil for 15 minutes. Transfer the eggs to the ice bath. When cool enough to handle, peel off the shells.

2. Halve the eggs lengthwise. Scoop out the yolks into a medium bowl. Set the whites aside.

3. Add the mayo, pickle relish, mustard, brown sugar, smoked paprika, and garlic powder to the egg yolks and mix well. Season with salt and pepper as desired.

4. Spoon the yolk mixture into a piping bag. Pipe some of the filling into each half of the egg white. (If you don't have a piping bag, you can just spoon the mixture into the egg whites.) Sprinkle with a dusting of smoked paprika and the bacon crumbles. Chill until ready to eat or serve right away.

Southern Inspired

Brunch's Best Breakfast Skillet | SERVES 4

I COULD'VE CALLED THIS DISH SUNSHINE SKILLET, because you'll feel the warmth and joy of a sunny day with that first bite. Sautéed potatoes, onions, peppers, sausage, bacon, and ham cradle cracked eggs in pockets before being blanketed in three kinds of cheese and baked in a cast iron skillet. Adjust the baking time for soft or firm yolks depending on your preference. Pure sunshine!

Southern Inspired

2 tablespoons vegetable oil

2½ cups medium-diced Yukon Gold potatoes

¼ cup medium-diced red onion

¼ cup medium-diced yellow bell pepper

Kosher salt for seasoning

Cracked black pepper

8 ounces ground breakfast sausage

1 cup cooked and crumbled bacon

¼ cup diced ham

6 large eggs

⅓ cup shredded mild cheddar cheese

⅓ cup shredded sharp cheddar cheese

⅓ cup shredded Monterey Jack cheese

Sliced scallions, for garnish

1. Preheat the oven to 350 degrees F.

2. Heat the oil in a large cast iron skillet over medium-high heat. Add the potatoes, onion, and bell pepper and season with salt and pepper as desired. Sauté the vegetables until soft, about 10 minutes.

3. Add the breakfast sausage and break it up with a wooden spoon to distribute it throughout the pan. Cook until the sausage is golden brown, about 4–5 minutes.

4. Add the crumbled bacon and diced ham, stir well, and sauté for about 5 more minutes.

5. With the back of your spoon, create 6 small indentations throughout the sautéed meat and vegetable mixture—each should be just big enough to hold an egg. Crack an egg into each indentation. Season with salt and pepper as desired.

6. Sprinkle the cheeses over the entire skillet. Pop in the oven for about 15 minutes or until the egg whites are cooked, the yolks are runny, and the cheese is melted.

7. Garnish with scallions and serve.

Biscuits and Brunch Party Gravy | SERVES 4

BISCUITS AND GRAVY are about as Southern as it gets, and this recipe builds upon that foundation with a more sophisticated flavor profile. Butter, shallots, ground sage, and crushed pepper add layers of flavor to the blond roux before the addition of Champagne and ground chicken or turkey—resulting in an extraordinary, rich, and creamy gravy. No Veuve in the wine fridge? Try substituting dry white wine or prosecco instead.

Biscuits	Party Gravy
2½ cups cake flour	3 tablespoons olive oil
1 tablespoon baking powder	1 pound ground chicken
¾ teaspoon kosher salt	Kosher salt
12 tablespoons (1½ sticks) unsalted butter, chilled and cut into small cubes	Cracked black pepper
	8 tablespoons (1 stick) unsalted butter
2 tablespoons cream cheese, chilled	1 large shallot, minced
2 tablespoons honey	1 tablespoon garlic powder
1¼ cups plus ½ teaspoon heavy cream	1 tablespoon smoked paprika
1 large egg	1 teaspoon dried sage
	1 teaspoon crushed red pepper
	½ teaspoon dried rosemary
	½ cup all-purpose flour
	1 cup Champagne
	2 cups no-sodium chicken broth

1. Preheat the oven to 400 degrees F and position a rack in the middle of the oven. Line a baking sheet with parchment paper.

2. In a large bowl, whisk together the cake flour, baking powder, and salt.

3. Add the butter, cream cheese, and honey. Using your fingers, break up the butter and cream cheese into smaller bits and incorporate into the dry ingredients. Your dough should look somewhat crumbly.

4. Push the flour mixture up again the sides of the bowl to create a well in the center. Add 1¼ cups of the heavy cream and gently combine the liquid

Southern Inspired

and flour mixture. You do not want to knead or mix with a spoon. It's best to use your fingers and lightly *fluff* around the mixture. This will help to avoid gluten formation and overworked dough.

5. Once the mixture starts coming together, pour it out onto a clean work surface and gently form a 1-inch-thick rectangle. Using a knife, cut 4 large biscuits and place on the lined baking sheet.

6. In a small bowl, whisk together the egg and remaining ½ teaspoon heavy cream and brush the mixture on top of the biscuits.

7. Bake the biscuits for 25–27 minutes or until the tops and bottoms are golden brown.

8. While the biscuits are baking, make the gravy. Heat the olive oil in a large sauté pan or skillet over medium-high heat. Add the ground chicken and cook, breaking it up into crumbles with the back of your spoon. Season with salt and pepper as desired. Cook until the chicken is cooked through and lightly golden brown, about 5–10 minutes. Pour off any excess liquid and transfer the chicken to a medium bowl.

9. In the same pan, melt the butter over medium heat. Add the shallot and season with the garlic powder, smoked paprika, sage, crushed red pepper, rosemary, and salt to taste. Cook until the shallot is translucent and aromatic, 1–2 minutes.

10. Whisk in the flour to thoroughly combine with the butter and shallot. Cook, whisking constantly, for 8–10 minutes over medium to medium-high heat to make a blond roux.

11. While whisking, pour in the Champagne and chicken broth until smooth. Bring the liquid to a light simmer over medium-high heat and let it cook until it begins to thicken into a gravy, 3–4 minutes.

12. Return the ground chicken to the pan and season to taste with salt and pepper.

13. Serve the gravy over the biscuits.

Mint and Honey Fruit Salad | SERVES 4-6

LET ME SHARE THREE TIPS for this salad with you: (1) Make sure you start with fresh fruit. (2) Follow the directions. (3) Don't keep this salad to yourself and eat it all at once—even though it's so good, you might want to! Brunch is supposed to be a *sharing* event.

2 tablespoons honey, divided	**1 cup diced honeydew**
1 cup diced pineapple	**1 cup diced strawberries**
1 cup diced cantaloupe	**Small bunch mint, stems removed**

1. Coat a large bowl with 1 tablespoon of the honey. Add the fruit and mix well.

2. Smack the mint leaves between your hands to release their oils. Tear or finely chop the mint and mix it with the fruit.

3. Drizzle the remaining 1 tablespoon honey on top, mix to combine, and serve.

Southern Inspired

Mason Jar Raspberry Chocolate Trifles | MAKES 4 TRIFLES; SERVES 4

THIS DESSERT IS A SENSORY DELIGHT! From its captivating colors of chocolate brown, crimson red, and milky white, to its bites of smooth, crunchy, and creamy, to its notes of tart and sweet—this dessert has it all. And the best part? It's super quick and easy to prepare. If you can't find raspberry pound cake, try a traditional butter variety instead.

½ cup chocolate fudge
8 ounces frozen whipped topping
1 (1-pound) loaf your favorite
    raspberry or plain pound cake,
    cut into medium to large chunks

1 cup raspberry jam
¾–1 cup crushed chocolate cookies
¼ cup caramel sauce

1. In a medium bowl, fold the chocolate fudge into the frozen whipped topping. The topping will deflate and that's OK! Stick the mixture back into the freezer to firm up for about 30 minutes.

2. Spoon the frozen whipped chocolate mixture into the bottoms of four pint-size mason jars. Add 3–4 pieces of cake on top, followed by some raspberry jam and crushed cookies. Repeat these steps about two more times (chocolate whipped topping, cake, raspberry jam, and cookies), ending with a fourth layer of chocolate whipped topping.

3. Drizzle the tops with caramel sauce and sprinkle with more crushed cookies.

4. Store in the refrigerator until ready to serve.

CHAPTER 11
Desserts TO DIE FOR
FROM MY MOMMA'S KITCHEN

*T*HERE'S AN ART TO LEMON-BASED DESSERTS. YOU WANT JUST enough bite to convince yourself that what you're tasting is more lemon than lemon-ish, but not so much that your eyes squint and your mouth twists into an uncontrollable pucker—that's never a good look. What you're aiming for is that perfectly balanced tangy, sweet spot.

My mom, Gwen, had the right lemon-touch when it came time to bake her strawberry lemon Bundt cake. What made this dessert so irresistible was her lemon glaze; she heated water and sugar to almost a simple syrup and then added butter and fresh lemon peel—that glaze wrapped around the cake like a warm blanket. But the party was just getting started, because inside the cake itself was a crimson surprise. She'd mix strawberries and sugar together, leaving the bowl in the fridge overnight to allow the mixture to develop a compote-like consistency, then she'd add it to the batter before baking. Luckily Gwen usually made three of these cakes at a time because as quickly as she'd make them, they'd be gone. A slice of that cake and a glass of cold milk always did the trick for me!

When I look back, I don't know if I enjoyed the cake or the batter more. You know what I mean—to a child, some batters taste just as good as (or even better than) the cake itself! But trust me, you'll want to bake my Mother of Love Strawberry Lemon Zest Bundt Cake. I hope you treat yourself and your loved ones to this and the other six Momma-inspired desserts in this chapter—Gwen would be so happy if you did!

Mother of Love Strawberry Lemon Zest Bundt Cake | SERVES 10

THIS IS ONE HAND-ME-DOWN that I didn't mind getting—hand-me-down recipe, that is. My mom, Gwen, got this one from her mom, and thankfully, she lovingly passed it down to me. First in beauty and taste, this fluffy and moist cake will cater to the tangy sweetness that only a lemon-berry combo can provide. Enjoy with tea, coffee, or better yet—a glass of cold milk.

12 tablespoons (1½ sticks) unsalted butter, softened
1 cup granulated sugar
½ cup honey or molasses
3 large eggs
2½ tablespoons fresh lemon juice
2 tablespoons lemon zest
2 teaspoons strawberry extract
½ teaspoon vanilla extract
2½ cups all-purpose flour
2 teaspoons baking powder
¼ teaspoon kosher or Himalayan salt

1 cup heavy cream
½ cup buttermilk
1⅓ cups small-diced strawberries, plus more berries for garnish
1 lemon, thinly sliced, for garnish

Lemon Glaze
1 cup confectioners' sugar
4 tablespoons (½ stick) unsalted butter, melted
¼ cup whole milk
1 tablespoon fresh lemon juice
1 teaspoon lemon extract

1. Preheat the oven to 350 degrees F. Grease a nonstick Bundt cake pan.

2. In a large bowl, cream together the butter and granulated sugar with a handheld mixer on medium-high speed until light and fluffy. Add the honey or molasses.

3. Add the eggs one at a time, blending well after each addition, then add the lemon juice, lemon zest, strawberry extract, and vanilla extract and incorporate well.

4. In a medium bowl, whisk together the flour, baking powder, and salt. Add a third of the flour mixture to the butter and mix on low speed to combine, being careful not to overmix.

Southern Inspired

5. In a small bowl, combine the cream and buttermilk. Add a third of the cream mixture to the batter and mix on low speed. Repeat until all the flour mixture and cream mixture have been incorporated. The batter will be on the thick side.

6. Gently fold the strawberries into the batter using a spoon or spatula.

7. Pour the batter into the prepared pan. Bake for about 1 hour or until a cake tester inserted in the center comes out clean.

8. Allow the cake to cool in the pan for about 20 minutes, then invert the cake onto a wire rack and cool completely.

9. Combine all the ingredients for the glaze in a small saucepan and heat over medium heat until it begins to simmer. Remove the pan from the heat and let the glaze cool slightly.

10. Pour the glaze over the top of the Bundt cake. Top with fresh strawberries and lemon slices—I think a combination of whole and sliced berries looks nice.

Granny Gwen's Banana Pudding | SERVES 8–10

MY MOM TAUGHT ME that your love shines through your food—whenever you put your hands and heart into making something, people can taste the difference. That meant that most, if not all, of her recipes were from scratch. There's something to be said for convenience, but there are volumes that can be shouted about homemade. That's why this banana pudding will take you *back home* with its silky-smooth homemade pudding base, cake-like texture of the wafers, and fresh whipped cream.

2 cups whole milk

1 (14-ounce) can sweetened condensed milk

¼ cup cornstarch

¼ teaspoon salt

1 large whole egg, plus 3 large egg yolks

2 tablespoons unsalted butter, cubed and chilled

¼ cup banana liqueur

1½ teaspoons vanilla extract

4 cups heavy cream, divided

½ cup confectioners' sugar

Juice of 2 medium lemons (optional)

6 ripe bananas, sliced on the bias

1½–2 (11-ounce) boxes mini vanilla wafers

1. In a medium saucepan, whisk the whole milk and condensed milk over medium heat until it begins to simmer.

2. In a large heatproof bowl, whisk the cornstarch, salt, whole egg, and egg yolks until the mixture is light yellow and smooth.

3. Once the milk mixture comes up to a low simmer, gently pour about 1 cup of the hot liquid into the egg mixture while whisking quickly and carefully. (Tempering the eggs will help keep them from scrambling.) Off the heat, pour all of the egg mixture into the pot with the milk mixture and whisk to combine.

4. Return the pot to the heat. Cook over medium-low heat, whisking constantly, until it thickens enough to coat the back of a spoon, 5–10 minutes. Remove the pan from the heat.

5. Stir or whisk in the butter, piece by piece.

6. Stir or whisk in the banana liqueur and vanilla until well combined.

Southern Inspired

7. Pour the pudding into a large bowl to quicken the cooling process. Put a piece of plastic wrap directly over the surface of the pudding to prevent a skin from forming. Refrigerate until completely chilled, about 1 hour.

8. Once you're ready to finish the pudding, start the whipped cream. Whip the cream in a large chilled bowl until medium peaks form. Slowly stream in the confectioners' sugar and juice of 1 lemon (if using) and continue to beat until stiff peaks form.

9. Once the pudding has chilled, gently fold half of the whipped cream into it. Reserve the other half for the topping.

10. If you like, squeeze the juice of 1 lemon over the banana slices in a bowl. This is optional, but it's nice if you want an extra-special presentation—the juice prevents the banana slices from becoming very brown.

11. Lay the vanilla wafers in an 8 × 12-inch ceramic or glass dish to cover the bottom. Carefully pour some of the banana pudding over the vanilla wafers and then layer on some of the bananas. Repeat each layer (cookies, pudding, and bananas) until you can't fit in anymore! Top with dollops of whipped cream and sprinkle with crushed vanilla cookies. If you happen to have any pudding left over, store in a glass container with a piece of plastic wrap pressed on the surface to prevent a skin from forming.

"Brown Sugar Baby" Peach Cobblers | SERVES 6

THIS RECIPE FEATURES THE THREE C'S—cobbler, cast iron, and comfort! It may also be one of the easiest and most satisfying home-made desserts that you can make. Let the juiciness of the peaches, the cakey crispiness of the crust, and the nostalgia of the mini cast iron skillets fill you with comfort as you take each bite. Served warm and topped with vanilla ice cream, this makes the perfect finale to your meal.

---

3 pounds sliced fresh or frozen peaches, plus more for garnish
Juice of 1 medium lemon
2 cups light brown sugar
1 tablespoon ground cinnamon
1½ teaspoons ground nutmeg
1 cup (2 sticks) unsalted butter, melted
2 cups all-purpose flour

2 tablespoons granulated sugar
2 teaspoons baking powder
2 cups whole milk
Ice cream, for serving

Topping
2 tablespoons light brown sugar
1 tablespoon ground cinnamon

---

1. Preheat the oven to 350 degrees F. Grease six 6-inch mini cast iron skillets.

2. In a large bowl, combine the peaches, lemon juice, brown sugar, cinnamon, and nutmeg and mix gently, making sure not to break down the peach slices. Pour the melted butter over the peach mixture and set aside.

3. In another large bowl, whisk together the flour, granulated sugar, and baking powder. Pour in the milk and mix gently until a smooth batter forms, making sure there are no lumps.

4. Divide the peach mixture evenly into the mini skillets. Spoon the batter by tablespoonfuls over the peach mixture in each.

5. To make the topping, mix the brown sugar and cinnamon together in a small bowl. Sprinkle about half of the cinnamon-sugar mixture on the cobblers, reserving the other half for after baking.

Southern Inspired

6. Bake for 35–45 minutes or until the tops are golden brown and the edges are bubbly. (You will know when they are done because the kitchen will smell like your grandma's house during the holiday!)

7. Remove the peach cobblers from the oven and sprinkle the remaining cinnamon-sugar on top. Cool slightly and serve with ice cream and additional peach slices if you wish.

Oatmeal, Chocolate, Raisin, and Almond Cookies | MAKES 24 COOKIES

DID YOU KNOW THAT MOST dark and golden raisins are made from the same variety of grape—Thompson seedless? What sets them apart is the way they're processed, giving each its unique flavor. I've used both varieties for this recipe and combined them with chocolate chunks and chopped almonds to deliver on taste *and* nutrition.

Southern Inspired

2 cups all-purpose flour

2 teaspoons baking powder

1 teaspoon ground cinnamon

½ teaspoon salt

Pinch ground nutmeg

1 cup (2 sticks) unsalted butter, softened

¾ cup light brown sugar

¾ cup granulated sugar

1½ teaspoons almond extract

½ teaspoon vanilla extract

2 large eggs

3 tablespoons milk

2 cups old-fashioned rolled oats

1 cup chocolate chunks

½ cup dark raisins

½ cup golden raisins

½ cup finely chopped almonds

1. Preheat the oven to 350 degrees F. Spray two rimmed baking sheets with nonstick spray or line with parchment paper.

2. In a medium bowl, whisk together the flour, baking powder, cinnamon, salt, and nutmeg.

3. In a large bowl, cream together the butter, brown sugar, and granulated sugar with a handheld mixer on medium speed until fluffy and airy. Add the almond extract, vanilla extract, eggs, and milk, and mix to combine.

4. Slowly add the flour mixture to the wet ingredients and beat until evenly combined.

5. Fold in the oats, chocolate, raisins, and almonds.

6. Use a tablespoon to shape the cookie dough balls. Drop the balls onto the prepared baking sheets, making sure they are 2–3 inches apart.

7. Bake for 10–12 minutes or until lightly golden brown. Remove the cookies to cooling racks. Allow the cookies to cool before serving. Store leftovers in an airtight container at room temperature.

Punch Bowl Cake | SERVES 6–8

THIS SOUTHERN DESSERT CLASSIC has remained a permanent fixture at our family gatherings—and for good reason. Equal parts tradition and taste, this dazzling dessert will captivate both young and old with its bold berry flavors bursting through bites of moist cake and creamy whipped cream. The key to making a boxed cake mix taste like homemade? Adding sugar and spice and everything nice, especially extra cake flour and butter. Nobody will believe it's not from scratch.

---

4 large egg whites
¼ cup granulated sugar
1 (15.25-ounce) package yellow cake mix
Water, eggs, and oil as needed per cake mix instructions
½ cup cake flour
8 tablespoons (1 stick) unsalted butter, melted
1 teaspoon vanilla extract

Mixed Fruit Layer
1 cup raspberries
1 cup blackberries
1 cup sliced strawberries
3 nectarines, pitted and sliced
½ cup granulated sugar

Whipped Cream
2½ cups heavy cream
Grated zest of 1 small lemon
¼ cup confectioners' sugar
2 tablespoons honey
1 teaspoon vanilla extract

---

1. Preheat the oven to 350 degrees F. Grease a 9 × 13-inch cake pan.

2. To make the meringue, beat the egg whites in a large bowl until stiff peaks form. Stream in the granulated sugar and beat just to combine.

3. In a stand mixer, prepare the yellow cake mix with the water, oil, and eggs according to the package instructions and mix until smooth. Add the cake flour and mix until smooth. Add the butter and vanilla and beat to combine.

4. Add a little bit of the meringue to the batter and mix, then fold in the rest. Gently tap the bowl against the counter to remove any large air bubbles.

(continued)

5. Pour the batter into the prepared pan. Bake for 38–40 minutes or until a toothpick inserted in the center comes out clean. Allow the cake to cool completely.

6. While the cake cools, combine the fruit in a large bowl and sprinkle with the granulated sugar. Stir well, then cover and allow to macerate in the fridge for about 30 minutes.

7. When you're just about ready to assemble the cake, make the whipped cream. In a chilled mixing bowl, whip the cream until medium peaks form. Add the lemon zest, confectioner's sugar, honey, and vanilla and continue to whip until stiff peaks form.

8. Gently slice off all the brown edges of the cake and cut it into large chunks. In your favorite punch bowl or trifle dish, layer some of the cake, followed by some of the whipped cream, and then some of the fruit in its syrupy liquid. Repeat each layer until you have reached the top and/or no more of the components are left.

9. Serve right away or chill until ready to enjoy!

Southern Inspired

Sweet Potato Pie | SERVES 8

YOU'LL FIND SEVERAL OF THESE PIES at every Thanksgiving celebration in our house. In fact, a sweet potato pie may just pop up at *any* time throughout the year in our house. The rich and velvety filling is courtesy of sweetened condensed milk and heavy cream, and is delicately flavored with nutmeg, cinnamon, and vanilla extract. Pie heaven!

---

3 medium to large sweet potatoes, peeled
1 premade (9-inch) pie crust
8 tablespoons (1 stick) unsalted butter, softened
¾ cup granulated sugar
½ cup light brown sugar

1 large egg, room temperature
1 (7-ounce) can sweetened condensed milk
½ cup heavy cream
1½ teaspoons vanilla extract
¾ teaspoon ground cinnamon
½ teaspoon ground nutmeg

---

1. Bring a medium saucepan of water to a boil over medium-high heat. Add the sweet potatoes and cook until they are tender and mashable, about 45 minutes. Drain, then return them to the pan over low heat to dry for 1–2 minutes. Make sure the potatoes do not form a skin. Cool completely, then transfer to a food processor or blender and puree (you should have about 2 cups).

2. Meanwhile, preheat the oven to the temperature recommended on the pie crust package. Place the pie crust in a 9-inch pie dish and crimp the edges to your liking. Spray the pie shell with a light coating of baking spray, poke it all over with a fork, and bake for 5–8 minutes. Set aside to cool. If necessary, turn the oven down to 350 degrees F.

3. In a large bowl, cream the butter, granulated sugar, and brown sugar together with a handheld or stand mixer on medium speed until fluffy.

4. Mix in the egg until just combined. Mix in the condensed milk, heavy cream, vanilla, cinnamon, and nutmeg.

5. Fold in the sweet potato until evenly incorporated. Pour the mixture into the parbaked pie crust and bake for 50–55 minutes, until the pie is nearly set in the center.

6. Remove from the oven and let the pie rest for at least 15 minutes, or allow it to cool completely before slicing.

Crunchy Peanut Butter Candy Ice Cream S'mores | SERVES 6

THIS IS WHY YOU HAVE TO save room for dessert! These scrumptious, mouthwatering ice cream sandwiches top the list of my favorite frozen treats. Not for the dessert-averse, these deliver on taste, texture, and indulgence. Just make sure all components are set and frozen before taking that first bite.

1 (7-ounce) can sweetened
   condensed milk
½ cup milk chocolate chips
½ cup miniature marshmallows
½ cup marshmallow fluff

12 whole graham crackers
½ cup chopped crunchy peanut
   butter candy bars
½ cup chopped pecans
½ gallon your favorite ice cream

1. Pour the condensed milk into a medium microwave-safe bowl. Microwave on high until it's runny, about 2½ minutes. (Alternatively, you can bring the milk to a light simmer in a double boiler on the stovetop. Be careful not to scorch the bottom.)

2. Stir in the milk chocolate chips until they have completely melted. Then stir in the mini marshmallows until completely smooth. Pour the mixture into a heatproof bowl to cool for 10 minutes. Fold in the marshmallow fluff.

3. Line a rimmed baking sheet with parchment paper. Spread the chocolate marshmallow mixture evenly on one side of each graham cracker. Sprinkle the crunchy peanut butter candy bar pieces and chopped pecans evenly on top. Transfer to the lined baking sheet. Freeze for about 30 minutes to let the s'mores set up.

4. Line another rimmed baking sheet with parchment paper. Remove the s'mores from the freezer. Scoop your favorite ice cream onto both sides of 6 crackers and spread in an even layer. Sandwich with the remaining 6 crackers, crunchy-side down. Transfer to the clean parchment paper and baking sheet and stick back in the freezer for at least 30 minutes or until ready to serve.

Southern Inspired

CHAPTER 12
Sippin'

*I*T HAS BEEN BOTH A JOY AND A PRIVILEGE TO SHARE MY MEMories and recipes with you throughout these pages, but now I'd like to share the story of a significant yet long-forgotten man who was deprived of his rightful legacy for more than a century. A man who defined American whiskey as we know it today. A man by the name of Nathan Green, or Uncle Nearest, as he was fondly called.

Uncle Nearest was an enslaved Black man who worked as a distiller for a preacher named Dan Call in the mid-1800s, in the small town of Lynchburg, Tennessee. During that time, Uncle Nearest developed a distilling technique whereby the whiskey was filtered through sugar maple charcoal prior to aging in charred oak barrels, allowing it to develop its signature smoothness—a technique specific to Tennessee whiskey, which is known as the "Lincoln County Process" and is still in use today.

Over the course of his enslavement, Uncle Nearest took on a young white apprentice by the name of Jasper Newton "Jack" Daniel and taught him everything he knew about distilling whiskey. Undeterred by the ugliness of slavery, the two developed a mutual respect that led to a true friendship. After Emancipation, Jack opened his own distillery and asked Uncle Nearest to work for him as his Master Distiller. Despite Uncle Nearest's contributions being eclipsed by time and forgotten memories, his significance was restored in 2017 when Fawn Weaver launched Uncle Nearest Premium Whiskey, the fastest-growing, independent, Black-owned, American whiskey brand in this country's history—and hired his great-great-granddaughter, Victoria Eady Butler, as its Master Blender.

As a personal tribute to this legend, I use Uncle Nearest Whiskey in my ultimate whiskey sour recipe. I hope you enjoy this and my five other alcoholic and nonalcoholic cocktails throughout this chapter, as you sip and spread some love.

Peach-Blackberry Mint Julep | SERVES 2

MY TAKE ON A TRADITIONAL MINT JULEP uses scotch instead of bourbon, giving it a deeper and smoother balance. Followed by sweet and tangy infusions of peach, blackberry, lime, and ever-present mint, this cocktail delivers on both taste and whimsy.

Mini ice cubes or crushed ice
4 ounces scotch
2 ounces peach puree
1 ounce fresh lime juice
2 mint leaves, torn, plus
    2 sprigs for garnish
4–6 blackberries, plus more
    for garnish
6 ounces lemon-lime soda

1. In a martini shaker combine some ice cubes with the scotch, peach puree, lime juice, torn mint leaves, and blackberries. Shake vigorously until the berries begin to break up. Pour the drink into two julep cups or other favorite glasses filled with mini ice cubes or crushed ice. Top each drink with lemon-lime soda and garnish with a mint sprig and more blackberries.

Southern Inspired

This Is *the* Whiskey Sour | SERVES 2

I USE UNCLE NEAREST 1884 WHISKEY to honor the man behind the name, and to honor you, my reader. The history and flavor of this 93 proof, small-batch whiskey, is unparalleled in taste and significance—and makes for an *impeccable* whiskey sour.

4 ounces Uncle Nearest 1884 Whiskey	2 ounces fresh lime juice
4 ounces simple syrup	Large ice cubes
2 ounces fresh lemon juice	Maraschino cherries, for garnish
	Lemon peel, for garnish

1. In a cocktail shaker, combine the whiskey, simple syrup, lemon juice, and lime juice with a cube of ice. Shake until everything is combined. Pour over a fresh ice cube in each of two glasses and garnish with maraschino cherries and lemon peel.

Get Your Life Right Party Punch | SERVES 18-20

I CONSIDER THIS A HEALTHY PUNCH—healthy for your reputation as a *party host extraordinaire*! It's almost impossible to feel anything but joy with a glass of this punch in hand. Five juices plus three spirits is the perfect equation for a Get Your Life Right party!

---

6 cups fruit punch
3 cups ginger ale
3 cups pineapple juice
2 cups peach juice
1 (12-ounce) can frozen lemonade
    concentrate
1 (12-ounce) can frozen orange juice
    concentrate

1 cup dark rum
1 cup light rum
½ cup grenadine
2 ounces Southern Comfort
Ice cubes
Orange slices, pineapple wedges,
    and maraschino cherries, for
    garnish

---

1. Mix all the ingredients together in a large pitcher, punch bowl, or drink dispenser. Garnish with fresh fruit on top of the punch and over the glasses. After one sip everything in your life will be right.

Granny Gwen's Party Rainbow Frappe | SERVES 18–20

I'M A GROWN MAN, BUT I'LL STILL HAVE a glass or two of this fizzy, fruity frappe whenever I attend a family get-together. This recipe is packed with creamy sherbet, refreshing juices, diced fruit, and meaningful nostalgia. Go ahead and break out that punch bowl with its dainty glasses for old times' sake—just try to avoid getting your fingers stuck in those tiny handles.

1 pint rainbow sherbet
½ cup raspberries
½ cup pineapple chunks
½ cup sliced strawberries
1 liter ginger ale
1 liter orange soda
1 liter lemon-lime soda
1 liter fruit punch
½ (6-ounce) can frozen orange juice concentrate, thawed
½ cup pineapple juice

1. Scoop the sherbet into a large bunch bowl and scatter the fruit on top. Pour over the remaining ingredients and stir. Serve individual portions using a ladle.

Southern Inspired

Citrusy Lime Margaritas | SERVES 2

A *GOOD* MARGARITA IS MADE WITH four basic ingredients: tequila, orange liqueur, lime juice, and ice. But the key to a *great* margarita is to make it with 100 percent blue agave tequila (as a bonus, quality tequila also helps you avoid a severe hangover), fresh lime juice for pop, triple sec for a balanced citrus punch, and crushed ice for shaking to allow for an optimum cocktail experience. You decide.

Crushed ice, for shaking
Juice of 4 limes, plus lime slices for garnish
6 ounces tequila

4 ounces triple sec
2 tablespoons turbinado sugar
2 tablespoons kosher salt
2 large ice cubes, for serving

---

1. In a cocktail shaker combine some crushed ice with the lime juice, tequila, and triple sec. Shake until the outside of the shaker is very cold.

2. Pour a couple of teaspoons of water into a small, shallow rimmed dish. In another small dish, combine the turbinado and salt. Dip the rims of two rocks glasses first into the water to moisten, then into the sweet salt mixture to coat.

3. Place 1 large ice cube into each glass. Strain the cocktail into the glasses and garnish with a lime slice.

Jernard's Georgia Pineapple-Ginger-Peach Slushy | SERVES 2-3

MAKE THIS RECIPE AS IS, OR OMIT the vodka for a fun and refreshing frozen mocktail. Can't find pineapple- or peach-flavored vodka? Plain vodka works just as well.

---

3 cups frozen peach slices

1½ cups frozen pineapple chunks

2 cups ice

4 ounces ginger beer

3 ounces peach-flavored vodka

2 ounces pineapple-flavored vodka

1 ounce pineapple juice

1 ounce simple syrup

Fresh grated ginger, for garnish

Fresh peach slices, for garnish

Fresh pineapple slices, for garnish

---

1. Combine the frozen peaches, pineapple, and ice in a blender. Pour in the ginger beer, vodkas, pineapple juice, and simple syrup. Cover and blend until smooth. If the slushy is thicker than you'd like, thin it out with more ginger beer. Pour into your favorite cocktail glasses and garnish with some grated ginger on top, a fresh peach slice, and a pineapple slice.

CHAPTER 13
Holiday

I’LL BE HONEST WITH YOU: MY FAMILY THINKS ABOUT THANKS-giving *all year long*. I mean it, as soon as one ends, we're already thinking about the next. That's something I got from my dad, Matt.

When November arrived, that tickle of anticipation would set in, and I'd feel a shift in energy. I knew the holiday season was about to kick off! That meant Thanksgiving prep was on everybody's mind. It also meant that Matt would be spending the next few weeks concocting new marinades or brines for the 10 to 15 turkeys that he'd be smoking and then frying out back. He'd experiment with different combinations of herbs, spices, sweet tea, cherry soda, cola, brown sugar, and even cognac. He marinated his turkeys for at least 48 hours before getting up at the crack of dawn on Thanksgiving morning to first smoke the birds over a low fire, then he and my great-grandfather would break out the giant cast iron cauldrons, deep like the ones used for frying cracklins, and fry those birds five at a time. The result was a beautifully crisped golden-brown turkey with a smoky bite—the best of two worlds.

But let's go back to the 10 to 15 turkeys. See, my dad loved people and was generous to a fault. On any given Thanksgiving we'd have anywhere between 35 and 50 people show up throughout the day. You know that phrase "go big or go home"? Well, every Thanksgiving we did it up big and everybody would go to *our* home! It was all good, all love!

I think my dad passed on his generosity gene to me, because my family and I still enjoy crowds of people during Thanksgiving. In fact, sometimes it feels more like a family reunion with all the people we entertain that day. And for those who can't make it, I prepare five to ten specialty turkeys that I share with them, but only if I've selected their names from the "Jernard Thanksgiving Turkey Lottery"!

Although Matt made memories with his deep-fried turkeys, I've adapted his flavors into a recipe that uses Cornish hens that can be easily fried in a large pot or home fryer. It would be an honor if you served my Fried Cornish Hens with Grandma's Corn Bread Dressing during your next holiday gathering; enjoy this and my other mains and sides as you break bread and bring fellowship to your table. Happy holidays and cheers to you!

Fried Cornish Hens with Grandma's Corn Bread Dressing | SERVES 4

SEASONED AND FRIED TO CRISPY PERFECTION and placed atop a bed of herbaceous savory dressing—or stuffing, as some people call it—these Cornish hens will take top honors for tenderness, flavor, and plating appeal at your holiday dinner table. Serve with my Roasted Root Vegetable Sheet Tray (page 227) to complete your memorable holiday meal.

Corn Bread Dressing
2 (8.5-ounce) boxes corn muffin mix
Eggs and milk as needed according to muffin mix directions
½ cup cornmeal
4 tablespoons (½ stick) unsalted butter, melted
1 bell pepper (any color), small diced
½ yellow onion, small diced
2 celery ribs, small diced
1 tablespoon dried sage
1 tablespoon dried rosemary
1 tablespoon dried thyme
1 tablespoon celery salt
1 cup chicken broth
1 (10.5-ounce) can cream of chicken soup

Fried Cornish Hens
Vegetable or peanut oil, for frying
1½ cups all-purpose flour
1 cup cornstarch
3 tablespoons fresh rosemary, plus several sprigs for garnish
3 tablespoons fresh thyme
3 tablespoons cracked black pepper
3 tablespoons smoked paprika
3 tablespoons garlic powder
3 tablespoons onion powder
1 teaspoon cayenne pepper
2 cups half-and-half
½ cup your favorite hot sauce, plus more for serving
4 Cornish hens
¼ cup honey

1. Preheat the oven to 400 degrees F. Grease a 9 × 13-inch baking pan.

2. In a large bowl, combine the muffin mix, eggs, and milk. Add the cornmeal and melted butter and mix well. Pour into the greased pan and bake for 20–25 minutes or until a toothpick inserted in the center comes out clean.

(continued)

3. Remove the corn bread from the oven and cool slightly. Transfer the corn bread to a large bowl. Add the remaining dressing ingredients and mix well, allowing the corn bread to crumble into chunks.

4. Pour the corn bread dressing mixture back into a greased baking pan and bake for 30–35 more minutes or until it sets. Set aside until ready to serve with the fried Cornish hens.

5. Pour oil into a large, heavy-bottomed pot to no more than halfway up the side. Prop or clip in a deep-fry thermometer so that the bulb is submerged in the oil. Heat over medium-high heat until the thermometer registers 350 degrees F. (Alternatively, you can use a deep fryer.) Set a wire rack in a large rimmed baking sheet.

6. In a large bowl or other container big enough to fit the Cornish hens, whisk together the flour, cornstarch, and seasonings. In another large bowl or container (same size), whisk together the half-and-half and hot sauce.

7. Dunk each Cornish hen into the half-and-half mixture and then dredge in the flour mixture.

8. Working in batches to not overcrowd the pot, gently lower the hens into the frying oil; you may have to adjust the heat on your stove because the oil temperature will drop tremendously when you add the hens. Fry until the hens are golden brown and crispy and reach an internal temperature of 165 degrees F, 15–20 minutes. Take the temperature in the thickest part of the thigh. Transfer the cooked hens to the rack.

9. Spoon the corn bread dressing onto a large platter and place the fried hens on top. Drizzle with more hot sauce and honey and garnish with fresh rosemary sprigs.

Note: Use the amount of eggs and milk that your corn muffin mix calls for.

Whipped Mashed Sweet Potatoes | SERVES 4–6

EASY TO PREPARE FOR SMALL OR LARGE CROWDS, this silky sweet potato side dish will add beautiful, rich color to your holiday lineup. Remember to boil your sweet potatoes in salted water to impart an added nuance of flavor.

Kosher salt

5 large sweet potatoes, peeled and
   diced

1 cup heavy cream

¼ cup light brown sugar

8 tablespoons (1 stick) unsalted
   butter

¼ cup maple syrup

2 teaspoons vanilla extract

2 teaspoons ground cinnamon

1 teaspoon ground nutmeg

¼ cup chopped walnuts, for garnish

1. Bring a large pot of salted water to a boil over medium-high heat. Add the sweet potatoes and cook until they are easily pierced through with a knife, about 15 minutes. Drain and set aside in a large bowl.

2. In a small saucepan, bring the heavy cream to a gentle simmer over medium heat. Add the sugar, butter, maple syrup, vanilla, cinnamon, and nutmeg and mix well.

3. Pour the warm liquid over the potatoes and gently use a whisk to whip until they are as lumpy or smooth as you like them to be.

4. Transfer the mashed potatoes to a serving vessel and sprinkle the top with the chopped walnuts.

BBQ Baked Salmon | SERVES 4–5

WHETHER YOU'RE TRYING YOUR HAND at a nontraditional holiday main or planning your Christmas Eve dinner, this BBQ Baked Salmon recipe is sure to satisfy your guests. Smoky-sweet homemade barbecue sauce flavored with ketchup, honey, Worcestershire sauce, chili powder, garlic, and lemon juice hugs the salmon as it bakes to perfection.

Honey Barbecue Sauce
½ cup ketchup
½ cup honey
¼ cup Worcestershire sauce
2 tablespoons minced garlic
1 tablespoon fresh lemon juice
1 tablespoon chili powder

2 tablespoons smoked paprika
1 teaspoon garlic powder

1 teaspoon onion powder
1 teaspoon lemon pepper
Kosher salt
Cracked black pepper
1 (2-pound) skin-on salmon fillet
Olive oil
1 teaspoon chopped fresh dill
Juice of 1 small lemon or lime, plus
  lemon or lime slices for garnish
  (optional)

1. Preheat the oven to 350 degrees F.

2. While the oven is preheating, prepare the sauce. In a medium saucepan, combine all the barbecue sauce ingredients. Bring to a simmer over medium-high heat, then set aside.

3. In a small bowl, mix the smoked paprika, garlic powder, onion powder, and lemon pepper and season with salt and pepper as desired. Place the salmon on a large rimmed baking sheet, rub with a drizzle of olive oil, and evenly season both sides with the spice mixture. Coat the salmon completely with the barbecue sauce.

4. Bake for about 15 minutes or until the desired doneness. Just make sure it reaches an internal temperature of 145 degrees F and the flesh is opaque and flakes easily with a fork.

5. Garnish the salmon with fresh dill and serve with lemon or lime slices on the side for squeezing, if you like.

Southern Inspired

Holiday Charcuterie Board | SERVES 6-8

WHEN I WAS GROWING UP, my great-grandfather, Peter Young, used to smoke his own cheeses and sausages in his backyard smokehouse. He was arranging charcuterie boards before we even knew there was a French word for *really good cheese and sausage plates.* As I grew and my palate matured, so did my love for this appetizer. The components of this board are meant to complement one another, but if you're unable to find a specific ingredient, try substituting a beloved favorite.

---

8 ounces Brie, Chaumes, or other soft-rind cow's milk cheese

6 ounces herbed Manchego

6 ounces Gorgonzola dolce

1 cup white cheddar cubes

4 ounces sliced salami

4 ounces sliced spicy salami

4 ounces sliced prosciutto

4 ounces thin breadsticks

4 ounces crostini

¼ cup organic sour cherry spread

1 bunch green grapes

½ cup grass-fed beef jerky pieces

½ cup lemon- and garlic-marinated olives, pitted

½ cup almonds, hazelnuts, and/or pecans

½ cup dried mango slices

¼ cup dried cranberries

Honey, for drizzling

---

1. Begin by laying the blocks of cheese on your board. Strategically place the sliced regular salami around the cheese. Wrap some of the breadsticks with prosciutto and spicy salami and lay them on the board along with additional breadsticks.

2. Fill in the gaps around the board with the remaining ingredients as you deem fit. Get creative with your charcuterie board!

Cheesy Collard and Mustard Green Bake | SERVES 4-6

THE BLENDING OF PEPPERY mustard greens with milder collard greens creates an effective base for this extra cheesy side dish. I usually serve this rich casserole at holiday get-togethers, but it also works as a party dip with crostini or breadsticks.

---

8 tablespoons (1 stick) unsalted butter

1 cup small-diced red bell pepper

2 tablespoons minced garlic

2 teaspoons crushed red pepper

Kosher salt

Cracked black pepper

1 pound collard greens, stemmed and chopped

1 pound mustard greens, stemmed and chopped

2 cups heavy cream

1 pound cream cheese, cut into chunks

¼ cup grated Parmesan cheese

4 cups shredded mozzarella, divided

---

1. Preheat the oven to 375 degrees F.

2. Melt the butter in a large saucepan over medium-high heat. Add the red bell pepper and garlic and sweat until the pepper is soft, 3–4 minutes. Season with the crushed red pepper and salt and pepper as desired.

3. Add the collard greens and mustard greens. Reduce the heat to medium and cook until almost wilted, about 10 minutes.

4. Add the heavy cream and cream cheese and bring to a simmer. Mix the cream cheese into the greens as it begins to melt.

5. Fold in the Parmesan and half of the mozzarella and mix until melted in.

6. Transfer the cheesy collard and mustard greens to a large baking dish. Top with more mozzarella cheese and bake for 10–15 minutes or until the cheese is melted and lightly golden brown.

Southern Inspired

Roasted Root Vegetable Sheet Tray | SERVES 4-6

ADD A KALEIDOSCOPE OF COLOR to your holiday menu with this recipe. Minutes to prep and under an hour to roast, this elegant collection of vegetables will help elevate your meal—especially with a sprinkling of truffle salt.

1 large orange sweet potato, sliced
1 large white sweet potato, sliced
2 yellow carrots, halved lengthwise
2 orange carrots, halved lengthwise
2 medium red beets, thickly sliced
2 medium golden beets, thickly
   sliced
4 medium purple potatoes, halved
1 cup marble potatoes

2 bunches radishes, halved
3 medium red onions, quartered
15 garlic cloves, peeled
Olive oil, for coating
1 teaspoon truffle salt (optional)
1 teaspoon cayenne pepper
Kosher salt
Cracked black pepper

1. Preheat the oven to 400 degrees F.

2. In a large bowl, toss the vegetables in enough oil to coat. Season with the truffle salt (if using), cayenne pepper, and salt and pepper as desired.

3. Spread the vegetables on a large rimmed baking sheet and roast for 40–45 minutes, until tender.

Acknowledgments

THIS BOOK IS A TESTAMENT TO MY COLLECTIVE VILLAGE, TO MY ancestors, and to the named and unnamed African American chefs who came before me. My road wasn't paved in gold but rather steeped in love, guidance, challenges, and grit. I'm *one* hardworking man, but I would not be where I am today without the support of *many*.

Let me start things off by giving thanks to the people who brought me into this world—my mom, Gwen, and my dad, Matt. Gwen, your unconditional love has allowed me to believe that I could reach for the stars and find my place at the table. And Dad, your legacy has been my inspiration and guiding light throughout this journey, and I am forever grateful to the two of you.

Thank you, Lil Momma and Peter Young, my great-grandparents. You taught me to love the land, love my roots, and love my community.

I don't know if there are enough words to express my thanks to my wife, Keena. Keena, we turned three months into 23 years and nine beautiful children. You've stood by me through the many falls, only to help me rise again with your endless love, support, and strength. You have fed my soul and encouraged me to pursue my dreams as we walk this earth together. You are my queen, my confidante, and my best friend. You are my everything, and I love you from the bottom of my heart!

To my right-hand man, Cory "Chef Romance" Hinton. Thank you for your commitment, perseverance, food styling savvy, and extensive culinary background while helping to develop and test these recipes. We walk in greatness, together!

Thank you, Carlos Scott, for believing in me. Your vision, courage and faith have helped make my dreams a reality—and we've only just begun!

Alan Morell and Tim Troke, thank you. I've always said that favor isn't fair but it's always right. Our partnership has manifested the birth of this book and countless blessings; our crossed paths were meant to be.

To my dynamic duo, Bill Hilary and Frankie Ordoubadi, thank you for your continued friendship and generosity as I walk toward my destiny.

I'd like to give an extra special thank you to the crew who did the heavy lifting on this book, my dream team at PowerHouse Productions. Thank you, Francesca Zani, for helping me organize, develop, test, and food style these recipes in the PowerHouse test kitchen. Jensen Taylor, thank you for your magnetic eye in capturing the most beautiful photos throughout these pages; your visuals brought color and joy to my storytelling. Thank you, Rochelle Brown-Johnson and Sonia Armstead, for your fierce and unwavering leadership in steering this project from concept to completion. As always, thank you, Kenneth "Kenny" Colbert and Sheila Wilson, for your ongoing support and enthusiasm. Your strength is my strength; your name says it all.

I'd like to give a big thank-you to my BenBella Books family, Glenn Yeffeth and Claire Schulz. Thank you for embracing my vison and bringing it to life on the written page.

To my mentors, Cathy Hughes and Rushion McDonald; I am humbled by your wisdom and grace. Thank you for your guidance and support as I become the man I'm meant to be.

Thank you, Dana Slusarenko. Friend of my friend who is now my friend— you have an amazing spirit and gift. I honor your talent for capturing my voice and expressing my essence. "Two are better than one; because they have a good return for their labor." (Ecclesiastes 4:9).

So much of what I do is for the next generations. Thank you to my children and grandchildren for shining bright: Jernard Wells Jr., Kameron Wells, Jasmine Wells, Jacobe' Wells, Carleisha Jones, Jamia Wells-Miller, Jalisa Wells, Zoe Wells, Keenan Wells, Reagan Petty, Kyrin Miller, Kyn'doll Miller, and Rhylee Jones.

Gratitude can't begin to express my many thanks to my loyal fans, family, and those who've helped me along the way: Michelle Rice, Alfred Liggins III, Robyn Greene Arrington, Jeff Meza, Rahsan Lindsay, Dr. Scott and Contessa Metcalfe, Burt Dubrow, Ali Dubrow, Linda Simmons, Mike Evans, Marquita Williams, Latonya Bryson, Adam Griffin, Shannon Williams, Towanda Cadoree, Anthony Griffin, Lester Potts, Mary Potts, Karen White, Apostle Christine Parker, Bishop Kevin Adams, Lisa Wells-Davis, Danny Wells, Keith Wells, Alvin Wells, Jackie Seals, Jermaine Seals, Erma Webber, Girtha Hoggs, Madie Sanders, Sam Banuelos, Matthew Berkowitz, Jordan Wiles, Mia Lloyd, Matt Ables, and the production staff at CLEO TV, TV One, and the Food Network.

And finally, a *big* thank-you to all those who told me I *couldn't*. Your unwitting contributions to my growth, both as a man and as a chef, have been *immeasurable*!

Metric Conversions

abbreviation key
tsp = teaspoon
tbsp = tablespoon
dsp = dessert spoon

u.s. standard . . . . . u.k.

1/4 tsp . . . . 1/4 tsp (scant)
1/2 tsp . . . . 1/2 tsp (scant)
3/4 tsp . . . . 1/2 tsp (rounded)
1 tsp . . . . 3/4 tsp (slightly rounded)
1 tbsp . . . . 21/2 tsp
1/4 cup . . . . 1/4 cup minus 1 dsp
1/3 cup . . . . 1/4 cup plus 1 tsp
1/2 cup . . . . 1/3 cup plus 2 dsp
2/3 cup . . . . 1/2 cup plus 1 tbsp
3/4 cup . . . . 1/2 cup plus 2 tbsp
1 cup . . . . 3/4 cup and 2 dsp

Index

JERNARD A. WELLS IS AN award-winning TV host, celebrity chef, and best-selling cookbook author. He is the host of *New Soul Kitchen* and *New Soul Kitchen Remix* on CLEO TV and is best known from numerous Food Network shows. Wells is also a contributor on *The Best Thing I Ever Ate* on Cooking Channel and *Food Fantasies* on Oprah Winfrey Network. He has worked with celebrities such as Tyler Perry, TV One founder Cathy Hughes, NBA All-Star Brandon Ingram, Tom Joyner, Bobby Brown, and Bell Biv DeVoe, to name a few. The James Beard House-honored chef is a two-time Telly Award winner and Taste Award winner. Wells is affectionately called the "Family Chef" and the "Chef of Love." He lives with his family in Atlanta, Georgia.